Strategies for a Successful Mealtime

Presented By:
Congressman Henry Cuellar
http://www.house.gov/cuellar

Strategies for a Successful Mealtime

**A Program for Children
with Autism Spectrum Disorder
and Related Disabilities
Who Have Eating Difficulties**

by

Maureen Flanagan, MA, CCC-SLP

Foreword by

Pamela J. Compart, M.D.

AAPC
PUBLISHING

©2016 AAPC Publishing
11209 Strang Line Road
Lenexa, Kansas 66215
www.aapcpublishing.net

Publisher's Cataloging-in-Publication

Flanagan, Maureen A.

  Strategies for a successful mealtime : a program for children with autism spectrum disorder and related disabilities who have eating difficulties / by Maureen Flanagan.
  Lenexa, Kansas : AAPC Publishing, [2016]

    pages ; cm.

        ISBN: 978-1-942197-13-3
        LCCN: 2015953300
        Includes bibliographical references.
        1. Eating disorders in children—Handbooks, manuals, etc. 2. Mastication disorders—Handbooks, manuals, etc. 3. Children—Nutrition—Psychological aspects—Handbooks, manuals, etc. 4. Psychomotor disorders in children—Handbooks, manuals, etc. 5. Perceptual-motor learning—Handbooks, manuals, etc. 6. Children with autism spectrum disorders—Treatment. 7. Autistic children—Treatment. 8. Teachers of children with disabilities—Handbooks, manuals, etc. 9. Parents of autistic children—Handbooks, manuals, etc.

RJ506.E18 F53 2016
618.92/8526—dc23

Black and white art and Photographs: ©iStockphoto; www.istockphoto.com and Maureen Flanagan ©2015

Sensory Gang ©Penny Chiles
This book is designed in Palatino.
Printed in the United States of America.

Dedication

This book is dedicated to my husband and daughters for their
never-ending support and encouragement.

Special thanks to the editing staff at AAPC for their guidance and assis-
tance, and to my daughter Julia, for her help with the photos.

– Maureen Flanagan

Table of Contents

Foreword

Feeding problems are extraordinarily common in children with developmental and behavioral challenges, particularly those children with autism spectrum disorders or significant sensory processing difficulties. As a developmental pediatrician in private practice who specializes in treating children with autism, I discuss feeding issues with families on an almost daily basis.

This book fills an important need by providing parents with an understanding of feeding problems and offering helpful, practical strategies.

This book begins with detailed explanations of the steps in typical development of feeding patterns at different ages. Reading about the intricate and sequential development of skills reminds us how truly remarkable it is that the majority of children eat without difficulty. Understanding where this developmental progression may go awry provides a basis for intervention in those children for whom typical feeding did not develop naturally. The early chapters of the book provide "red flags" for parents that may be signs that feeding problems are present or emerging.

This book also makes an important contribution in correctly emphasizing the importance of the child's sensory system in relation to food refusals. Children with autism may reject food for a variety of reasons such as its taste, smell, texture, or visual appearance. It is important to remember that the child's perception is his reality, and any therapy must first meet the child where he is and progress from there. Feeding is not just a coordinated motor activity; it is also a sensory experience. This book provides an approach that focuses on the combination of both aspects. It is an important resource in helping parents understand their child's feeding issues both from a developmental perspective but also, very importantly, from a sensory perspective.

In an ideal world, every child with a feeding issue would have access to a speech pathologist, occupational therapist or behavioral therapist with expertise in treating feeding issues. Access may be limited for a number of reasons: 1) Availability of appropriately trained therapists locally; 2) Financial issues affecting affordability of services, especially if they are not covered by the family's insurance; and 3) Logistical issues (e.g., availability of appointment times that are accessible given a parent's work schedule or a child's school or nap schedule). For all of these reasons, a book that can provide parents with a clear understanding of the underlying issues and a program they can institute at home fills an important need.

Even with access to an appropriate therapist, feeding issues require more than just treatment in the therapist's office. Each mealtime offers the opportunity for carry-over of the in-office treatment plan to real-life settings (home, school). The more all parties involved are educated about a particular child's specific feeding program, the more success can be achieved. This book provides important information that will help parents and other providers better understand the principles underlying a feeding program which is the basis for practical interventions.

Maureen's book provides in-depth explanations of the various factors which can affect the experience of feeding as well as specific interventions to address and overcome these factors. She supplements this with real-life examples from her clinical experience; many parents will undoubtedly see their children in these examples. This book has clearly been a labor of love by an experienced clinician with decades of experience in treating feeding disorders in children with developmental challenges and is a helpful resource for both parents and clinicians alike.

Pamela J. Compart, M.D.

Developmental Pediatrician

HeartLight Healing Arts

www.heartlighthealingarts.com

Introduction

- Charlie loved chicken nuggets shaped like animals and ate them every day for lunch. One day, his mother gave him chicken nuggets that were not shaped liked animals, and Charlie refused to eat them. They looked different and were, to him, not chicken nuggets.

- Austin ate a turkey sandwich on toasted bread every day for lunch at school. One day, his mother cut the sandwich into different shapes. Austin refused to eat it. It had become a new food because it no longer looked like the food that he was used to eating every day for lunch.

- Mark ate only one variety of applesauce and did not accept any other brands even though the appearance and texture were the same.

- James chewed on a chew tube, a mouth tool used to help with jaw stability throughout his day. When offered solid foods to chew, he only chewed one brand of potato chips. He screamed when offered any other crunchy, soft, or hard solid.

- John ate a wide variety of foods but now will only eat pasta with a specific brand of Italian dressing.

- Andrew ate lunch at home but refused to eat lunch at school.

- Mary put a variety of food in her mouth. She held the food in her left cheek cavity and did not swallow it.

- Sally only ate dry cereal and crackers. As a result, her mom did not look forward to food shopping or mealtimes.

- Harry ate red apples every day for a month but then one day suddenly refused to eat them anymore.

- "My son would only eat the most minuscule amount (of food), not enough to give it a chance. He would say "no, yuck, yuck." He was terrified of food, terrified of the unknown taste. He was also scared of the noise food made in his head" (Legge, 2002, p. 194).

The children in these opening vignettes all have a diagnosis of autism spectrum disorder (ASD). ASD is listed in the *Diagnostic and Statistical Manual of Mental Disorders* (DSM-5; American Psychiatric Association, 2013) as a neurodevelopmental disorder characterized by persistent deficits in social communication and social interactions and restricted, repetitive patterns of behaviors, interests, or activities. Included in the new diagnostic criteria under the category of **restricted, repetitive patterns of behavior, interests, or activities** is the following: "hyper- or hypo-reactivity to sensory input or unusual interest in sensory aspects of the environment" (p. 50). This includes unpleasant responses to sounds and textures and extreme smelling and touching and, therefore, is related to feeding and eating.

Given this background, it is important for all who live or work with a child with ASD to be aware of the possibility that behaviors observed at mealtime may be a reflection of characteristics of the disorder rather than "volitional acts of noncompliance" (Twachtman-Reilly, Amaral, & Zebrowski, 2008, p. 262).

Processing and Integrating Sensory Information and Novel Stimuli

As illustrated in the examples given, many children with ASD have difficulties with eating, including aversion to taste, smell, texture, food type, color, freshness, and temperature as well as acceptance of only specific mealtime utensils (Bruns & Thompson, 2011; Legge). In some instances, the appearance of food may cause a child to reject food without even tasting it (Williams & Seiverling, 2010). In addition, some have a fear of anything new or unfamiliar and therefore an aversion to trying anything new (Thornton, 2003).

In attempts to explain the causes of these reactions and, ultimately, come up with effective interventions, several researchers (Ayres, 2000; Courchesne, Lincoln, Kilman, & Galambos, 1985; Dawson, 1989) have noted that many children with a diagnosis of autism do not demonstrate an adaptive orienting response to novel stimuli, which may cause an aversion response and a failure to process novel stimuli, including new foods. This was supported in a report by Corbett and colleagues that concluded that children with ASD reacted to novel stimuli in an unusual manner, resulting in exaggerated cortisol responses (Corbett, Mendoza, Abdull, Weyelin, & Levine, 2006).

Along with difficulty processing novel stimuli, children with ASD are, to varying degrees, unable to register and modulate sensory information in one or more of the sensory systems (Ayres; Henry & Myles, 2014; Yack, Aquilla, & Sutton, 2015). This makes it difficult to plan, initiate, and sequence movements and to develop an oral feedback system. The end result is a lack of or poor development of the underlying components of movement, which in turn affects the child's eating, speech, and communication skills (Flanagan, 2008).

The typical brain integrates the sensory information it takes in and then acts upon it. The ability to integrate sensory information is often diminished in children with ASD. Ayres, in her book *Sensory Integration and the Child*, documented the symptoms of poor sensory processing that can affect oral-motor development in children with ASD. These children have difficulty controlling sensory input, which causes them to receive either too much input or not enough. They are unable to balance the input they receive (Henry & Myles). As a result, they may overreact to noise, have an aversion to physical contact such as hugging, dressing, or getting their hair washed or combed as well as reject new foods and various tastes, smells, and textures. If they become overstimulated, they may over- or underreact and become defensive (Flanagan).

King (1991) estimated that 85%–90% of children with ASD have sensory integration challenges. Tomchek and Dunn (2007) supported this prevalence of sensory processing disorder in children with ASD. These children may function typically in some areas, but in other areas they experience sensory-based, often extreme, fears. We see this behavior in many of the vignettes in the introduction, such as the boy who was afraid of the taste of the food and the sounds that the food might make and, as a result, rejected it after only a small taste.

In order to understand how a dysfunction related to processing information through one of the sensory systems affects how a child might react, it is important to know the sensory systems, their locations, and functions. This information is presented in Table A.1 and will help with comprehension of the sensory systems.

Table A.1
Location and Functions of the Sensory Systems

System	Location	Function
Tactile (touch)	**Skin** – density of cell distribution varies throughout the body. Areas of greatest density include mouth, hands, and genitals.	Provides information about the environment and object qualities (touch, pressure, texture, hard, soft, sharp, dull, heat, cold, pain).
Vestibular (balance)	**Inner ear** – stimulated by head movements and input from other senses, especially visual.	Provides information about where our body is in space, and whether or not we or our surroundings are moving. Tells about speed and direction of movement.
Proprioception (body awareness)	**Muscles and joints** – activated by muscle contractions and movement.	Provides information about where a certain body part is and how it is moving.
Visual (sight)	**Retina of the eye** – stimulated by light.	Provides information about objects and persons. Helps us define boundaries as we move through time and space.
Auditory (hearing)	**Inner ear** – stimulated by air/ sound waves.	Provides information about sounds in the environment (loud, soft, high, low, near, far).
Gustatory (taste)	**Chemical receptors in the tongue** – closely entwined with the olfactory (smell) system.	Provides information about different types of taste (sweet, sour, bitter, salty, spicy).
Olfactory (smell)	**Chemical receptors in the nasal structure** – closely associated with the gustatory system.	Provides information about different types of smell (musty, acrid, putrid, flowery, pungent).
Interoception (inside body)	**Inside of your body** – helps the body "feel" the internal state or conditions of the body.	Provides information such as pain, body temperature, itch, sexual arousal, hunger and thirst. It also helps bring in information regarding heart and breathing rates and when we need to use the bathroom.

From Sensory Issues and High-Functioning Autism Spectrum and Related Disorders: Practical Solutions for Making Sense of the World by B. S. Myles, K. Mahler, and L. A. Robbins. Copyright 2014 AAPC Publishing. Shawnee Mission, KS: AAPC Publishing. Used with permission.

Eating issues often start in infancy. Based on data collected by questionnaires from the Avon Longitudinal Study of Parents and Children, Edmond, Emmett, Steer, and Golding (2010) reported that "children with ASD showed feeding difficulties from infancy and had a less varied diet from 15 months of age," (p. e337). Furthermore, children later diagnosed with ASD were shown to be introduced to solids after the typical 6 months of age, were described as "slow eaters," and were reported to be "difficult to feed," (p.e337). Other symptoms, such as pickiness and a limited acceptance of food types and textures, were also observed in some children prior to their diagnosis of autism. Edmond et al. suggested that infants and toddlers with feeding issues and refusal of a variety of food types should be screened for other behaviors associated with autism such as social communication skills, joint attention, and repetitive behaviors. Indeed, others have observed that problems with eating can be seen as part of the repertoire of symptoms for a child with ASD (Twachtman-Reilly et al.).

Feeding/Eating Disorder as a Sensory-Motor Disorder

As illustrated, a feeding disorder is a sensory-motor disorder and should be treated accordingly. This involves analyzing the child's oral movement patterns as well as his ability to register and regulate sensory information. Sensory input through planned activities will help the child control his reactions to sensory information and improve his behavioral response (Yack et al.).

That is where this book comes in. This book provides a structured oral-motor and feeding program as well as an understanding of the underlying movement patterns that influence the child's ability to eat and drink a variety of foods. Through use of the program described in this book, parents and professionals will be able to help the child register (notice and pay attention to), regulate (modulate or control the sensory input), integrate (assimilate to form a clear perception of the sensation), and organize ("put it all together") sensory input. Table A.2 gives examples of how a child might register, regulate, integrate, and organize sensory information.

Table A.2
Characteristics of Sensory Integration

Register	Regulate	Integrate	Organize
"I smell something" (Olfactory System)	"I smelled it before"	"It is maple syrup"	"Yummy good"
"I feel something" (Tactile System)	"It is touching my arm but it is not scary"	"It is my mom touching me"	"I can keep eating"

Overview of the Book

- My son is 12 years old and still has major feeding issues (Sayers, 2008).

- My son will be 4 this year (nonverbal), and he will only eat baby food, certain crackers, and French fries and has a hard time feeding himself.

- My 3½-year-old daughter with a diagnosis of ASD also has a great number of sensory issues and difficulty eating certain foods.

- My son is 11 years old and was diagnosed with Asperger's syndrome several years ago. His hostility toward every meal I placed before him caused me the greatest amount of anguish (Legge, p. 9).

Feeding skills and behaviors can be changed over a period of time as long as a step-by-step program is consistently followed with the child. This book informs parents, teachers, and other caretakers of what such a program should look like for a child. Specifically, the goal of this book is to help parents and teachers understand how a child's sensory challenges and difficulties producing typical oral movement patterns can affect her ability to accept textured foods, a variety of foods, and novel foods.

Knowledge of typical oral, feeding, and texture development is essential in order to determine if a child is showing a delay in oral and feeding skills, exhibiting primitive movement patterns, or demonstrating skills that are generally not seen in typical development. Therefore, Chapter One outlines typical feeding, oral, and texture development. Given the sensory nature of eating problems, Chapter Two discusses the sensory systems and how processing of information through these systems can affect the child's feeding skills. Specific sensory-motor activities are presented in Chapter Three, designed to help the child regulate his responses to a variety of sensory information to make for a successful mealtime. Chapter Four explains how to modify the mealtime environment for success. Assessment of the child's feeding skills is essential prior to designing an individual treatment program. Chapter Five describes the assessment process. Intervention should occur in small steps that follow typical development but begin at that child's current skill level. Chapter Six presents information on treatment in a simple-to-follow, structured manner so that parents, teachers, and other caretakers can implement it with the child/children in their care. Chapter Seven emphasizes how sensory activities must be part of the routine of both home and school to ensure generalization and greater success with the goals addressed during the feeding program. It presents a variety of activities that parents, teachers, and other caretakers can incorporate into the child's routines that will facilitate improved feeding skills. Finally, Chapter Eight summarizes the important points made throughout the book.

> **NOTE:** To be inclusive, the pronouns "he" and "she" are alternated within and across chapters when referring to children with ASD.

Chapter 1

Typical and Atypical Feeding Development

CHAPTER PREVIEW

Typical Feeding Development

Components of Oral Movement

Stages of Texture Development

Oral Movement Patterns Causing Concern

This chapter presents a review of the oral movement patterns that are produced in typical eating/feeding development as well as red flags suggesting areas of concern. Armed with this knowledge, parents and caretakers as well as teachers, therapists, and other professionals will be better able to provide treatment.

As illustrated in the Introduction, many children with ASD have difficulty processing and integrating novel stimuli, which may cause difficulty with the acceptance of new foods, textured foods, and foods already part of a diet that have changed in appearance. This chapter presents the typical development of texture as well as the movement patterns needed to be successful at each level of texture. Furthermore, the movement patterns that are a cause for concern are labeled and defined with regard to how they may affect the child's ability to produce mature movement patterns. This information will assist with the development of a structured approach to changing the texture and appearance of foods to ensure a higher chance of acceptance into the child's diet.

Typical Feeding Development

Knowing what happens during each stage of typical feeding development helps us to know the child's level of functioning and, consequently, develop appropriate treatment programs. For example, a child may not have the oral movement patterns necessary to chew a hard, solid food that is presented to him. Perhaps he is functioning at a lower level of development than expected for his age and does not yet have the jaw stability to adequately chew a solid food. Such a child may need to practice with lumpy or ground foods as well as soft solids before he is ready to chew a hard solid.

Oral Movement Components

The following components or parts of oral movements are essential for the development of mature movement patterns:

1. Reflexes
2. Oral awareness
3. Oral discrimination
4. Oral stability
5. Separation of movement
6. Grading of movement
7. Combining/sequencing of movements

These components are discussed in the following sections as they develop at each stage, from birth to 36 months.

Reflexive Stage: Birth to 3 Months

The child uses reflexive movement patterns—automatic movements that are not under the child's control—to give protection and function to a system that is not capable of volitional or purposeful movement. An example of a reflexive movement pattern giving function to the child's system is the automatic suck pattern produced when the lips are stimulated by touch. This allows the child to bring food into her mouth before she is capable of actively moving her mouth. As the child matures, each reflex is integrated and becomes the basis for further development. This means that the child is no longer controlled by these automatic movements but has control over the movements and can produce them on his own. For example, at 4–6 months of age, the child can hold the mouth open for the spoon or nipple. After the food or liquid is taken into the mouth, the child then initiates a forward/backward tongue movement in coordination with his breathing. The child now has control over the movement patterns that were previously automatic.

The child's ability to receive and respond to touch stimulation is important for the development of early reflexes and the ability to produce coordinated sucking, swallowing, and breathing (Bodison, Hsu, Hurtubise, & Surfus, 2010).

Oral reflexes present in the newborn include:

- **Rooting reflex:** The infant turns her head toward the side that is being touched and opens her mouth (Upledger, 1996). Rooting is a food-seeking, survival response.

Rooting reflex.

- **Suckle-swallow reflex:** The infant begins to suck when the center or sides of the lips, cheeks, or inside of the mouth are touched. This is another survival response because it allows the child to move his mouth in order to take in food even though he does not yet have active control over oral movements (Evans-Morris & Dunn-Klein, 2000).

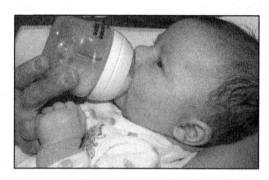

Rhythmical suck/swallow with a bottle while engaged with person feeding him.

- **Babkin palmomental reflex:** When pressure is applied to the middle of the infant's right or left palm, she opens her mouth and bends toward the respective side of her body. This assists with survival as a food-seeking response and oral exploration, which is crucial for the development of tongue movement (Evans-Morris & Dunn-Klein, 2000). Oral exploration assists with enhancement of oral awareness and oral discrimination. These two components of sensory-motor development are essential for the maturity of tongue and lip movements during the feeding process.

- **Phasic bite reflex:** This is an up/down movement of the jaw prompted by touching the cheeks or gums. It is a rhythmical pumping movement of the jaw for food intake (Beckman, 1995b). Another purpose of this and the other oral reflexes is to protect the child's airway (McCarthy, 2008).

Characteristics of Typical Movement and Structures from *Birth to 3 Months*

- Lower jaw is small and retracted and oral cavity is small.
- Jaw, lips, and tongue move as one unit.
- Tongue movement is forward/backward as the tongue fills the oral cavity.
- Breathing is nasal to allow breathing/swallowing at same time due to anatomy until 3–4 months.
- Infant drinks 2–4 oz. every 3–4 hours (Ernsperger & Stegen-Hanson, 2004).

Causes for Concern

- **The child's reflexes are not present, observed on one side of the body but not on the other, or are difficult to stimulate.** Reflexes should be symmetrical, active, and easily stimulated.
- **The child's movements are not rhythmical.** Movements should be smooth and rhythmical. "Rhythm is the most consistent characteristic of feeding patterns during the first three months of life" (Evans-Morris & Dunn-Klein, 2000, p. 20).
- **The child stops and starts with the sucking pattern or has difficulty initiating the sucking pattern.** Sucking is typically one suck/swallow per second in infants. These movements should be constant and rhythmical.
- **The child uses one side of the body or oral system more than the other.** There should be symmetry within the system.
- **The child's tongue has a bunched, thick configuration, which often signals difficulty with suck/swallow.** There should be a flat, cupped tongue configuration with a groove down the middle of the tongue to guide the liquid to the back of the mouth for the swallow.

Development of Oral Awareness: 4–6 Months

In the typical population, eating takes less time at this stage of development because the oral reflexes are no longer present and oral awareness, oral discrimination, and oral stability have begun to develop. Along with the development of purposeful movement, there is exploration with and of the oral structures (lips, tongue, face). That is, the child is learning about different sizes, shapes, and textures. It is the beginning of the child's oral feedback system as she starts to develop controlled movements. The child puts fingers, clothes, and toys in her mouth. Such active exploration with the tongue, lips and jaw are important for developing oral awareness and oral discrimination. Prior to this stage, her movements were reflexive, and he was unable to change how she moved her mouth. All her movements were the same. Now, she can begin to feel and change her mouth movements depending on what is being put in her mouth. All of this is occurring while the child is also developing the ability to hold her head in the middle and her lower jaw is growing downward, allowing for more space in the mouth. These changes in the child's oral system are occurring at the same time that there are changes with her gross- and fine-motor skills. This, in turn, enables more movement of the jaw, tongue, and lips as the child explores her environment.

At this stage of development, the time the child spends eating should be an enjoyable, interactive time with parents and caretakers.

Characteristics of Typical Movements and Structures at 4–6 *Months*

Increased oral space:

- The infant must now coordinate suck/swallow with breathing.
- The infant begins to develop an up/down tongue movement during the swallow, but we still see the forward/backward tongue movement with the swallow that was present at birth to 3 months.
- The infant has increased tongue and lip movements during play with hands and objects to mouth. This means that the tongue is exploring outside of the oral cavity.

Increased oral stability:

- The infant is able to maintain an open, quiet mouth for the spoon. However, there is a wide mouth opening—that is, control of lower jaw movements is just beginning to develop.

- The infant has active center lip movement on the nipple.

- The infant has increased liquid intake, drinking 7–8 oz during four to six feedings a day.

- The infant produces a munching pattern with soft solids. This is an up/down movement of the lower jaw with a spreading/flattening of the tongue. The whole mouth is moving together while munching.

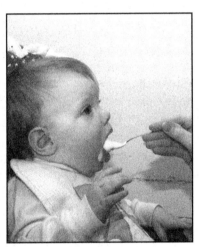

Maintains an open mouth for the spoon.

Causes for Concern

- **The child does not go through this stage of oral exploration.** Parents often report that their child with ASD did not orally explore his environment at 4–6 months. *(oral awareness)*

- **The child has difficulty accepting solid food.** At this age, Edmond et al. (2010) found that children later diagnosed with ASD had difficulty accepting solid foods and were characterized as "slow feeders." *(oral awareness and oral discrimination)*

- **The child does not move her tongue outside of her mouth.** Children with a diagnosis of ASD may not move their tongue outside of their mouth. This is due to poor oral tactile awareness and discrimination. *(oral awareness and oral discrimination)*

- **The child does not increase liquid intake during the four to six feedings each day.** In the typical population, the speed of feeding increases at this stage of development because of the integration of oral reflexes, and the development of oral awareness, oral discrimination, and oral stability. Because the child with ASD may not develop the necessary amount of awareness, discrimination, and stability, the speed of feeding may not be sufficient to increase fluid intake. *(oral awareness, oral discrimination, and oral stability)*

Continued Development of Oral Awareness and Discrimination: 7–9 Months

The child is continuing to explore the sensory features of objects with the oral system: size, shape, texture, taste (Ernsperger & Stegen-Hanson). The child is developing a concept of herself by exploring her world visually, orally, and motorically (Salek, 1975). She is exploring new foods with her eyes, ears, hands, and nose before putting it in her mouth (Potock, 2010). The child's mouth structures are increasing in stability and separation, which is important for the maturation of oral skills (Evans-Morris & Dunn-Klein). As the child's jaw becomes more stable, the tongue and lips are able to move separately from the lower jaw. This allows for faster and more controlled movements. The child at this stage is easily accepting a range of new foods with varied tastes, textures, and appearances.

Characteristics of Typical Movements and Structures at 7–9 Months

Increased oral awareness and discrimination:
- The child is tolerating lumps and textures in ground foods and mashed table foods. This helps to prepare the child for future success with eating a variety of table foods.
- The child is eating finger foods (Evans-Morris & Dunn-Klein).

Increased stability and separation of tongue/lips:

- The child's postural stability has increased, as seen through the child's ability to sit independently and begin to creep and crawl.
- The child's body develops stability, and the tongue and lips begin to move separately from the jaw.
- The child produces a tongue lag during the swallow. The tongue remains on the top of the mouth for a split second while the lower jaw drops down. This is the first sensation or sign of separate tongue movement.
- The child is able to transfer food to side or middle of the mouth.
- The child has separate, lateral tongue movements, movements to the side gums. Tongue lateralization begins with gross rolling movement or horizontal shifts of the tongue to the side.
- The child uses separate, downward upper-lip movement to clean the spoon.
- The child bites pieces of soft solids.
- The child drinks from the bottle without spilling.
- The child can take one to three sips from a cup; there is still liquid loss from the cup.
- The child uses up/down, variable jaw movements while chewing. This shows that the reflexive movements have integrated and more mature movements are developing.
- The child can produce long strings of sounds separate from movement.
- The child has increased interaction and play during mealtime.

Takes one to three sips from a cup.

Causes for Concern

- **The child refuses mashed or ground junior foods or table food.** These are foods with lumps that are not uniform in size. He only accepts one soft, smooth food type *(oral discrimination)*. Such refusal is often reported with children with ASD who have feeding issues.

- **The child is still losing liquid while drinking from a bottle.** *(oral stability)*

- **The child demonstrates no lip movement downward onto the spoon to assist with cleaning the spoon.** (separation of movement)

- **The child refuses drinking from a cup** *(oral stability)*. Some parents of children with ASD report that their child refuses to drink from a cup or only drinks out of one specific cup.

Beginning Development of Graded Movement: 10–12 Months

Graded movement refers to the ability to control the size and amount of movement produced by the oral structures. Stability, graded movements, and separation of movements are easily observed in the child's movements at this stage of development. The child's oral stability and separation of movement continue to develop and form a basis for the ability to begin to grade movements.

The child is open to learning new skills with a cup and spoon. She is not restricted to drinking liquids from only a single cup or bottle or only using a particular spoon or dish. The child is open to trying new foods.

Characteristics of Typical Movements and Structures at *10–12 Months*

Graded movements:

- The child has a more controlled bite on a soft cookie.
- The child uses minimal jaw movements while drinking long sequences from a bottle.
- The child uses graded and separate upper-lip movements for cleaning the spoon.

- The child draws in the lower lip to clean the lip with graded mouth opening.

Stability and separation of movement:
- The child moves food from the center, to the side, to the center for swallowing.
- The child uses separate movements of the cheeks to keep food from falling into cheeks. This is the start of elevated tongue tip while swallowing semi-solids and solids (Evans-Morris & Dunn-Klein, 2000).
- The child has improved drinking with the bottle.
- The child holds the cup back in the mouth for stability.
- The child demonstrates up/down excursions of the lower jaw with the cup.
- The child loses liquid, especially as cup is removed from the mouth.
- The child frequently coughs when drinking thinner liquids from the cup.

Causes for Concern

- **The child drinks from only one cup or bottle** (*oral awareness and oral discrimination*). As stated previously, some children with ASD only drink from one specific cup or bottle. Any change with this can cause the liquid to be rejected by the child.
- **The child makes poor use of the lips to clean the spoon and lips.** *(oral awareness and separation of movement)*
- **The child spills liquid with the bottle.** *(oral stability)*
- **The child has difficulty keeping the food on the teeth edges and moving it to the teeth edges for chewing.** *(separation of movement)*
- **The child resists chewing soft solids** (*oral stability and oral discrimination*). Children with ASD may reject soft solids, particularly if it is a new food. Some children only eat a smooth, puréed food type.

Improved Stability, Separation of Movement, and Grading of Movement: 13–15 Months

Oral skills become more refined with improved stability, separation of movement, and grading of movement. Also, at this stage of development, the child's feeding skills become more independent.

Characteristics of Typical Movements and Structures at 13–15 Months

Increased stability of the oral system:

- The child's drinking skills improve. There is no liquid loss with removal of the cup. The child is able to sequence three sip/swallow sequences from the cup.
- The child's chewing skills mature as seen through diagonal movements of the jaw.
- The child produces mature tongue movements with the spoon. Up/down tongue movements replace forward/backward tongue movements with a spoon food. With this change in tongue movement, less food is coming out of the mouth during spoon feeding.

Increased separation of tongue/lips from jaw:

- The child's cheeks and lip corners draw inward for food placement and transfer.
- The child uses the upper incisors to clean the lower lip.
- The child is able to lift the tip of tongue for exploration of the top of the mouth.

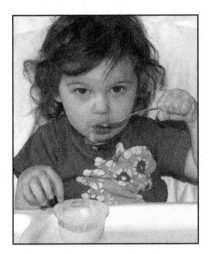

Separate lip movement on the spoon.

Causes for Concern

- **The child is not able to smoothly transfer food to the side for chewing.** *(oral stability and separation of movement)*

- **The child shows no independent lip movement.** *(oral stability and separation of movement)*

- **The child has difficulty facilitating pleasurable, independent eating skills** *(oral awareness, oral discrimination, oral stability, and separation of movement).* Many parents with a child with ASD report how difficult mealtimes are, with their child rejecting most foods.

- **The child continues to be a messy eater** *(oral awareness and oral discrimination).* Children with ASD may continue to be messy eaters because of their poor processing of touch.

- **The child spills liquid while drinking from a cup.** *(oral stability)*

- **The child demonstrates poor ability to sequence sip/swallows from a cup.** The child with ASD may only be able to take one sip at a time due to difficulty with sequencing movements. *(sequencing movements)*

Greater Control of Oral Movements and Independence: 16–18 Months

The increased control is due to continued improvement in stability, separation of movement, and grading of movement. Evidence of this increased control is seen by the child's ability to bite through a hard solid with the absence of head movement. This shows independence of jaw movement from head and shoulder movement and more controlled use of jaw.

Characteristics of Typical Movements and Structures at 16–18 Months

Further development with self-feeding:

- The child has independent cup drinking skills. He is able to swallow with lip closure and tongue tip movement and use separate upper lip movement onto the cup edge.

- The child's chewing skills mature as seen through the ability to bite through a hard cookie with a sustained bite due to graded biting force or pressure.

- The child feeds herself through finger feeding. She is able to chew with lips closed depending on the food type. Children at this stage of development generally want to feed themselves.

Able to chew with lip closure.

- The child is able to eat soft solids from a spoon and uses forward/downward upper lip movement to clean the spoon. The ability to draw in the lower and upper lips shows increased separation of the upper and lower lips from the jaw. The child is also developing hand skills, which assist with the ability to independently eat from a utensil (Bodison et al.).

Causes for Concern

- **The child has difficulty biting through a hard cookie.** Parents with a child with ASD often report that the child only likes crunchy solids or foods that require no chewing, such as pasta. *(oral stability and grading of movement)*

- **The child does not want to feed self. Children at this stage are becoming very independent and tend to only eat foods that they can feed themselves.** Children with ASD may struggle with the use of utensils, making it difficult to feed themselves. *(separation and grading of movement)*

- **The child lacks awareness of food on lips or face.** This poor awareness is indicative of poor tactile perception and discrimination. According to the DSM-5, there may be hyper- or hypo-reactivity to sensory input with a diagnosis of ASD (American Psychiatric Association). Hypo-reactivity of sensory input would hinder awareness of food on the lips or face. *(oral awareness and oral discrimination)*

Increased Separation of Movements and Combination/Sequencing of Movements: 19–24 Months

The child demonstrates a variety of combinations of lip, tongue, and jaw movements due to greater variety of foods eaten (Evans-Morris & Dunn-Klein). Also, there is a fluid combination of movements. The child can clean the upper lip with his tongue and smoothly bring the tongue in to swallow food. Jaw stability continues to develop. Due to increased jaw stability, internal jaw stabilization develops at this stage—the child can hold the cup on the lip edge. He no longer needs to hold the cup back in the mouth to help stabilize the jaw while drinking. Up/down movements of the lower jaw are no longer present while drinking.

Characteristics of Typical Movements and Structures from *19–24 Months*

Greater separation of tongue from jaw:

- The child elevates the tongue blade, tip, and front of the tongue with side-to-side transfer of food across the midline.
- The child uses the tongue tip to clean the cheek and gum area. Child can move the tongue tip separately from the tongue blade.
- The child elevates the tongue to clean the upper lip.

Jaw stability:

- The child is able to eat firmer meats.
- The child is able to elevate the tongue tip due to increased stabilization of the jaw.
- The child drinks long sequences from the cup.
- There is no liquid loss from the cup.
- The child is able to drink from a straw.
- The child begins to use internal jaw stabilization while drinking from a cup.

Increased jaw stability allows eating more solids. *Drinks from a straw.*

Causes for Concern

- **The child lacks experience with a variety of food types and liquids.** As stated throughout this book, many children with ASD struggle with new foods. This opposition limits the repertoire of foods and liquids accepted by them. *(oral awareness and oral discrimination)*

- **The child spills liquid from cup with wide jaw movements while drinking.** *(oral stability)*

- **The child is unable to drink from a straw.** The child with a diagnosis of ASD may be resistant to trying a straw. Some children are resistant to using anything different or new. *(oral discrimination, separation and grading of movement)*

- **The child lacks tongue tip definition and separate tongue tip movement to clean the lips, teeth, and gums.** *(separation of movement)*

- **The child is unable to transfer food from side to side across midline.** *(separation of movement)*

- **The child lacks fluid, sequenced movements, jaw stability, and separation of lip and tongue movement from jaw movement.** Some children with ASD have difficulty with sequencing movement patterns. This characteristic may cause difficulty with sequencing movements while eating at this stage of development. As stated in the introduction, increased movement patterns of the jaw, lips, and tongue develop as the child eats a greater variety of foods. If the child with ASD is opposed to trying new foods with a variety of textures, these movement patterns may not develop. *(sequencing of movements)*

Precise and Rhythmical Movements with Increased Speed: 24–36 Months

Children produce rhythmical movements with increased speed and precision. Further developments at this stage include single movements, observed at earlier stages of development, now combined to form sequenced movement patterns that are used by the child during the process of eating. Mealtimes should be pleasurable. These experiences lay the foundation for the acceptance of a variety of future mealtime experiences.

Characteristics of Typical Movements and Structures at *24–36 Months*

Mature chewing patterns:

- The child is able to bite through most foods with graded jaw movements, including meats and raw vegetables.
- The child easily transfers food from side to side with tongue tip.
- The child, at 36 months, is able to transfer food upon request and uses a circular-rotary jaw movement.
- The child maintains lip closure while chewing.

Increased speed and precision of movements:

- The child uses the tongue to clean the lips and cheeks with increased speed and precision.
- The child's cleaning movements are smoothly integrated with chewing (Evans-Morris & Dunn-Klein).

Mature drinking patterns:

- The child drinks from a cup with internal jaw stabilization.
- The child produces elevated and independent tongue tip movement for the swallow (Evans-Morris & Dunn-Klein).

Drinking with internal jaw stabilization.

Causes for Concern

- **The child cannot transfer food to either side of the mouth upon request.** As noted in the introduction, children with ASD may have difficulty motor planning their movements. While the child may be able to transfer food to either side of the mouth when he is not thinking about doing this skill, this may become difficult when requested by somebody else. *(sequenced movements)*

- **The child is stuffing food in the mouth and is a messy eater.** This is often seen with a child with a diagnosis of ASD due to poor processing of tactile information. The child does not receive the sensation that her mouth is full or that her face has food on it. *(oral awareness and oral discrimination)*

- **The child produces wide vertical jaw movements with food loss while chewing.** *(oral stability, separation of movements and grading of movements)*

As discussed under the stages of development, the typically developing child also goes through a sequence of acceptance of food textures. This information is reviewed, expanded upon, and illustrated in the next section.

Stages of Texture Development

The child's level of oral-motor skills must be considered when new textures are introduced. This section defines the various food textures and reviews the stage of development when each texture is accepted and the movements necessary for success (Ernsperger & Stegen-Henson).

Thin Purée: 4–6 Months

A thin puree is a thin paste or liquid made with a blender or strainer.

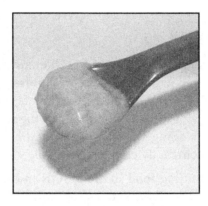

Oral movements required to eat thin purée:

- Integration of the oral reflexes: The child can produce movement on his own

- Ability to open the mouth for the spoon

- Increased oral awareness: This occurs as the child explores hand, feet and objects with his lips and tongue

- Forward/backward tongue movements with the spoon: The tongue is still moving front to back in the mouth rather than up and down

Thick Purée: 6 Months

This is defined as a thicker, smooth food without lumps. Examples include blended meats, fruits, vegetables, and thickened cereals.

Oral movements required to eat thick purée:

- Ability to hold the mouth open and use upper-lip movement to clean the spoon
- Forward/backward tongue movements with the spoon
- Tolerance for increased sensation on tongue as thicker food drops onto the tongue
- Tolerance for thicker food without gagging

Mashed Lumpy Foods: 7–9 Months

This is defined as food that is blended or mashed and forms a thick consistency with lumps. These include mashed table foods such as mashed bananas, mashed carrots, mashed potatoes, and mashed sweet potatoes.

Oral movements required to eat mashed lumpy foods:

- Increased play with toys and fingers in the mouth and exploration of the tongue outside of the mouth
- Increased separation of movement:
  a. The upper lip moves downward and forward to clean the spoon
  b. The tongue moves to the side gums
  c. The tongue stays at the top of the mouth for a second before dropping down to the lower jaw; this is called a "tongue lag"

Ground Food: 7–9 Months

This is defined as food with lumps that are not uniform in size. Examples of this are scrambled eggs, ground beef and cottage cheese.

Oral movements required to eat ground food:

- Vertical chewing movements: no longer using a combination of the phasic bite pattern and sucking movements
- Lateral tongue movement
- Some active lip movement with jaw movement

Chopped Table Foods: 12 Months

This is defined as table foods that are cut into quarter- to half-inch pieces such as fruit cocktail, small pieces of cereal, sliced bananas, cut-up toasted wheat bread, diced soft meats, and cut-up vegetables.

Oral movements required to eat chopped table foods:

- Controlled bite on soft foods: the child can control the size of the mouth opening and the amount of pressure needed to bite on a soft solid

- Increased ability to transfer food from side to center to side to assist with chewing and swallowing.

Oral Movement Patterns Causing Concern

At each stage of development from birth through 36 months, movements or behaviors that were cause for concern were previously described. In this section these are further defined and broken down into three categories: delayed development, primitive movement patterns, and atypical movement patterns.

Delayed Development

The term "delayed development" indicates that the child is developing the same skills as his typical peers and in the same sequence but at a slower rate (Flanagan).

If the child is continuing to use external jaw stabilization (holding the cup edge back in the mouth or biting on the cup edge) past 19–24 months, this indicates that her movement pattern is delayed. Delayed development of oral stability inhibits the increase in skills typically produced from 19 to 36 months, such as the ability to combine and sequence movements, separating tongue and lip movements from jaw movement, and biting through most foods.

External jaw stabilization: holding the cup back in the mouth to help stabilize the cup while drinking.

Primitive Movement Patterns

These movement patterns are seen in a typically developing infant from birth to 6 months. The presence of the following reflexes past 6 months of age would be considered a primitive pattern:

- Strong rooting reflex
- Phasic bite reflex
- Suck/swallow reflex
- Babkin palomental reflex

The presence of these reflexes inhibits the development of mature movement patterns. For example, the child who continues to exhibit the Babkin reflex may reflexively open his mouth any time he bears his weight on his hands or holds something in his hand. This interferes with the ability to produce purposeful mouth movements.

Disordered/Atypical Movements

These are movements that would not be seen in the child's typical peers.

Low muscle tone. Children with ASD often exhibit low muscle tone. Low muscle tone means that the muscles are slow to contract or do not fully contract, making it difficult to maintain muscle contraction for as long as would be expected (Gagnon). The child may have difficulty sitting upright in a chair for long periods of time and exhibit poor control of the oral musculature due to a slowness to respond and poor contraction of the musculature. An example of poor control of the oral musculature would be difficulty using the upper lip to clean food from the spoon.

Slow, imprecise and weak movements of the oral musculature is called dysarthria. This will inhibit the typical development of feeding skills (Beckman, 1995a). Children exhibiting dysarthria may also show signs of apraxia—that is, the "inability to voluntarily combine, organize and sequence movements" (Kumin, 2002, p. 11).

Children who have difficulty planning and sequencing also have difficulty predicting what might happen next. A child who insists on eating the same food prepared the same way at each meal may be attempting to increase the predictability of the mealtime experience because predicting is difficult for them (Twachtman-Reilly et al.). This enables them to better know what will happen at each meal.

Poor registering of and difficulty modulating sensory input (Flanagan). This means that the child has difficulty paying attention to and controlling sensory information. Children with ASD, to varying degrees, show difficulty paying attention to, controlling, and responding to sensory information, which results in hypo- or hyper-response to sensory stimulation (Ayres). This in turn causes the child to crave some sensory stimuli and avoid others. Indeed, 85%–90% percent of children with a diagnosis of autism have sensory integration problems (Edelson, 1996); that is, they are unable to effectively organize sensations for use (Ayres). Tomchek and Dunn also found a high incidence of sensory integration issues in children with ASD.

Research has shown that these atypical behaviors are a result of "neurobiological differences" (Twachtman-Reilly et al.). These differences directly impact the child's ability to eat a variety of food types due to difficulty registering and modulating responses to tastes, smells, and tactile input. Twachtman-Reilly et al. found a correlation between taste accuracy and acceptance of textures and flavors. A child who is under-reactive to tastes, smells, and tactile input may choose foods with very strong flavors to stimulate her oral receptors, whereas a child who is over-reactive may choose foods that are bland (Bruns & Thompson). Escalona, Field, Singer-Strunck,

Cullen, and Hartshorn (2001) found that many children with ASD exhibit excessive sensitivity to touch, causing them to be on the alert and making it difficult for them to attend to what is important to pay attention to at any moment. Because the tactile system, the first sensory system to develop, is important for survival (Yack et al.), these children are in survival mode. The child might spend his time in the cafeteria worried about who might touch him and not be able to focus on his lunch.

Inconsistent reactions. The responses to sensory information may change over the course of the day depending on the amount of sensory information processed by the child, making it difficult to predict how the child will respond to a given situation. The child's responses may erroneously be seen as volitional. It is important to effectively observe and interpret these responses as a result of an atypical sensory processing system (Twachtman-Reilly et al.).

Compensatory Patterns

Compensatory movement patterns may develop as the child attempts to function in spite of the sensory-motor difficulties (Flanagan). An example of a compensatory movement pattern would be the child moving the lower jaw forward or to the side to compensate for tight muscles of the neck and poor stability of the lower jaw. These tight muscles would restrict the movement of the lower jaw and so the child would need to find another way to move the lower jaw. Children with this poor jaw stability and these tight neck muscles may further compensate by only wanting crunchy solids that are easier to chew or foods that can be easily swallowed without chewing, such as pasta or puréed foods.

Compensatory movements can also develop with over-reactivity or hypersensitivity to touch. The child might react defensively to touch around and inside the mouth, causing her to clench her jaw. Under-reactivity or hyposensitivity to touch might result in an intense need to touch everything or a lack of desire to touch anything not familiar (Hoekman, 2005). Both of these reactions to tactile information would impede oral movements during eating by affecting motor planning and the ability to sequence or combine movements (Nadon, Feldman Ehrmann, Dunn, & Gisel, 2011).

This chapter identifies typical and atypical patterns of movement. In addition, red flags or "cause for concern" at each stage of development are specifically explained as they might relate to children with ASD. They are further characterized as delayed development, primitive movement patterns, and atypical movement patterns. Equipped with this information, parents, caretakers, teachers, and therapists should be better prepared to decide whether to refer a child in their care for a feeding evaluation.

Chapter 2

A Sensory-Motor Approach

In order for mealtimes to be successful, the child needs to be advancing toward a state of calm and alertness, capable of organizing sensory information and developing a feedback system (King). The information in this chapter will help parents, caretakers, teachers, and therapists understand how difficulty with various sensory channels may be causing disorganization within the child (Myles, Mahler, & Robbins, 2014) and, consequently, trouble interacting with his mealtime environment. Specifically, hypo-reactions, hyper-reactions, and fluctuating responses are described for each of the senses. These can influence the child's feeding skills by causing atypical perceptions with regard to food textures, tastes, smells, sounds, and visual as well as novel stimuli. These uncharacteristic perceptions, in turn, may make it difficult for the child to predict what will happen next, with the result that the child rejects much of the food and drink placed before her, leading to a very limited diet (Twachtman-Reilly et al.).

Tactile System

The tactile or touch system is the system that sends stimulation to the central nervous system through receptors in the skin. These receptors register light touch, pressure, pain, heat, and cold. The light touch receptors are an alerting, protective sense designed to make us check on what might be touching us. Other touch receptors tell us what we are touching. The third set of touch receptors obtains information about heat, cold, and pain (Edelson). These neural receptors prepare our bodies in case there is a need for either flight or fight (Ayres).

The tactile system, which is the first system to develop *in utero*, is important for survival and development. Many of the newborn reflexes are stimulated through touch. For example, the baby turns his head toward touch in order to find the nipple, opens his mouth following stimulation to the palm of his hand, and begins to suck/swallow following stimulation to the tongue and palate.

As the system matures and becomes less reflexive, the touch discrimination system begins to develop as the child explores her environment and develops a balance between protective and discriminative touch. For example, the baby knows when touch is alarming, when it can be ignored, and when it is pleasurable (Yack et al.).

Some children with ASD do not develop this balance between protective and discriminative touch due to atypical processing of information through the tactile system, causing their responses to be hypo-reactive, hyper-reactive, and/or fluctuating.

Hypo-Reactive Responses

Children who are hypo-reactive or under-reactive to touch require more intense input in order to indicate touch. This interferes with the development of body awareness and the ability to motor plan movements because the child is not receiving accurate feedback from his tactile system. This leads to poor oral awareness and oral discrimination and, as a result, difficulty discriminating between food textures, which in turn may cause the child to reject new foods, ultimately leading to a limited diet and possible health issues (Nadon et al.).

Other behaviors frequently noted in children with an oral system that is hypo-reactive to touch include eating nonedible objects, overstuffing the mouth, and excessive messiness while eating (Twachtman-Reilly et al.) because they may not feel the food on their faces or in their mouths. There may also be buildup of saliva in the mouth due to poor oral awareness, which could cause drooling and difficulty swallowing. Children with a hypoactive tactile system have low arousal levels leading them to excessively touch "everything" in order to get adequate amounts of information to their nervous systems. This may also be why some children eat inedible objects; these objects provide tactile input that is strong enough for the child to register the information (Yack et al.).

Finally, due to poor body awareness and motor planning difficulties, the child may have trouble controlling lip and tongue movements, which can interfere with the development of mature movement patterns (Flanagan). In short, an under-reactive tactile system negatively affects the development of the motor system and the ability to further develop oral motor, feeding, speech, and language skills. This child will not get the sensation of separate tongue and lip movement while eating that we see develop at 7–9 months because her mouth is so full of food.

POOR ORAL AWARENESS ▶ **STUFFS FOOD** ▶ **NO SEPARATE LIP/TONGUE MOVEMENT**

Hyper-Reactive Responses

A child with a hyper-reactive tactile system shows an excessive reaction to touch. Such a child is often on alert in a primitive flight, fight, or freeze state, making it difficult for him to attend to people and objects in his environment. Since this child may be in an alert state, he may find it difficult to eat in a crowded and noisy environment, such as a school cafeteria. He may react by becoming aggressive (fight), by trying to leave the environment (flight), or by shutting down and refusing to eat anything (freeze) (Twacht-man-Reilly et al.).

This child may react negatively and emotionally to touch because her oral discrimination system is not reading touch accurately (Ayres). Harmless touch may be interpreted as potentially dangerous. Poor oral awareness and discrimination also inhibit her ability to develop mature lip and tongue movements. If she does not tolerate thicker, lumpy foods, these mature movement patterns may not develop. Separate and up/down tongue movements develop as the texture of food increases.

DEFENSIVE TO TEXTURE ▶ **ONLY EATS SMOOTH FOODS** ▶ **NO SEPARATE TONGUE MOVEMENT**

A child with a hyper-reactive response to tactile input may refuse foods due to sensitivities to food textures and temperatures and reject utensils because of the way they feel inside of his mouth (Rogers, Magill-Evans, & Rempel, 2011). One parent reported that her son does not clean the spoon when given a bite of anything and does not like to feed himself. Food on his face and hands causes distress and inhibits his desire to eat. He often wants to have his shirt changed if food spills on it.

Another parent noted that her son eats in the front of his mouth and runs to the toilet to spit food out. This may be because the child does not like the way food feels when it touches his tongue. This can also interfere with teeth brushing. There are many sensory receptors on the face, lips, tongue, and hands compared to the rest of the body. This is why these specific areas are so often involved in behavioral challenges for the child who has tactile sensitivities (Escalona, et. al).

TACTILE SYSTEM

Hyper–Reactive Responses	Hypo–Reactive Responses
Reacts negatively to touch	Requires intense touch input
Sensitive to food textures/temperatures	Lacks oral awareness and motor planning
Refuses some food types	Stuffs food/messy eater
	Eats inedible objects

Vestibular System

The vestibular system is located in the inner ear. It tells us where we are in space. This system enables us to maintain muscle tone, hold ourselves upright against gravity, sustain balance, plan our movements; and coordinate head, eye, and body movements (Flanagan). This sensory system plays an important role in modulating all the sensory systems and regulating our behavior because it has many interconnections with many parts of the brain (Ayres). As such, it affects the part of the brain that controls our ability to stay alert and focused.

The vestibular system functions at both a protective and a discriminative level. For example, movements can stimulate reflexes to protect the newborn. Later on the vestibular system helps us to discriminate between fast or slow movements (Yack et al.). It is also closely related to the auditory system (King, 2007–2008).

Children with ASD tend to have difficulty processing information from the vestibular system. They may be over- or under-reactive to vestibular input (Hoekman).

Hypo-Reactive Responses

The child who is under-reactive to vestibular input may be in constant motion—spinning, jumping, falling, and bumping into things (Flanagan)—to maintain an adequate level of arousal and organization. Clearly, these behaviors make it difficult to maintain attention to a task such as sitting at the table during a meal. Such a child, therefore, may be walking around the table with her dinner or constantly rocking in her chair. In addition, the child may have difficulty controlling, planning, and grading her movements (Yack et al.). Poor grading of jaw movements while chewing, inadequate lip movements for cleaning a spoon, and poor tongue movement for transferring food may result from hypo-reactivity to vestibular input.

The vestibular system also affects muscle tone. Poor muscle tone makes it difficult to maintain an upright sitting posture while eating a meal. The child may be concentrating so much on maintaining an upright position in the chair that he cannot focus on anything else. Therefore, the child may compensate by eating with his head on the table and find it difficult to use utensils, tending instead to eat with his fingers rather than using a spoon or fork.

Hyper-Reactive Responses

The child who is hyper-reactive to vestibular input may avoid excessive movement and may experience motion sickness in the car or on a swing (Flanagan). The child may also be fearful of sitting in an unsupported chair. She is afraid of falling, which would stimulate the vestibular system (Twachtman-Reilly et al.).

VESTIBULAR SYSTEM

Hyper-Reactive Responses	Hypo-Reactive Responses
Avoids excessive movement	Uses constant movement for arousal/ organization
Fears unsupported position	Uses utensils poorly
Avoids use of utensils	Has poor sitting posture due to low muscle tone

 # Proprioceptive System

The proprioceptive system gives us subconscious awareness of our body position and changes in our position in space through sensory receptors in our muscles, joints, and tendons (King, 2009). An intact proprioceptive system enables our bodies to adjust to our position in space. This helps us to stay seated in a chair or walk down the stairs (Hoekman); it also gives our muscles information on how much force is needed to grade our movements appropriately. Furthermore, the body awareness we get from the proprioceptive system also assists with the ability to sequence, organize, and execute movements.

An intact proprioceptive system helps us feel safe and calm (Flanagan) and can regulate our body's state of arousal and can help decrease hyper-reactive responses to other sensory information, challenges that many children with ASD face. Many of the functions of the proprioceptive system overlap with the functions of the vestibular system (Yack et al.).

Hypo-Reactive Responses

A child who has hypo-reactive responses to proprioceptive input exhibits poor body awareness in space, messy eating, and difficulty manipulating small objects. He may seek additional proprioceptive input by purposely falling down, banging into walls or objects, leaning against others, or touching walls while walking down the hall. This sensory-seeking behavior may also be the child's way to help decrease hypersensitivity to other sensory input and/or an attempt to regulate his nervous system.

The child with hypo-reactive responses to proprioceptive input has difficulty grading and planning her oral movements during mealtimes. For example, she may open her mouth wider than necessary for the spoon or solids and have difficulty knowing how much force to use to chew different solids. Problems with holding and using utensils may be an issue during the meal (Nadon et al.).

Hyper-Reactive Responses

A child who has hyper-reactive responses to proprioceptive input exhibits many of the same characteristics as the child with a hypo-reactive proprioceptive system, including a lack of awareness of body in space, clumsiness, frequent falling, difficulty manipulating small objects, and messy eating. The child also has difficulty predicting how to grade and plan the movements necessary for new foods and, therefore, typically rejects the new food and continues to eat only the known foods. These hyper-reactive responses to proprioceptive input are often associated with hyperactive responses of the tactile or vestibular systems.

PROPRIOCEPTIVE SYSTEM

Hyper-Reactive Responses	Hypo-Reactive Responses
Lacks body awareness	Lacks body awareness
Difficult with grading and planning movements	Difficulty with grading and planning of movements
Prefers known foods/avoids new food	Prefers known foods/avoids new foods
Hyper-reactive tactile and vestibular systems	Hypo-reactive tactile and vestibular systems

🐨 Auditory System

The auditory system includes our ears and our central auditory pathways, which end in the temporal lobes of the brain. This consists of the outer ear, middle ear, inner ear, and the central nervous system (Yost, 2002).

The auditory system is responsible for receiving, encoding, transmitting, and decoding sound signals. It also analyzes the sound and filters out unnecessary information (Lawrence, 1971).

Hypo-Reactive Responses

The child who has hypo-reactive responses to auditory information may appear not to hear sounds or directions. The noisy environment of the school cafeteria, for example, may be challenging for this child. He may not be able to filter out the important sounds, like speech, from the unimportant background noises. Therefore, the child may shut down during the meal and have difficulty eating because of being overwhelmed by competing stimuli. This is not the same as being hyperactive to sounds. This child is shutting down because he cannot filter competing sounds that should remain in the background.

Hyper-Reactive Responses

The child who is hyper-responsive to auditory information may react negatively to sounds by crying, covering her ears, or becoming aggressive. Competing auditory information for this child might stimulate the fight-flight-freeze reflex, causing the child to fight, run from the area, or withdraw (Twachtman-Reilly et al.). The child may be sensitive only to certain sounds such as high-pitched noises and loud or sudden sounds (Ernsperger & Stegen-Hanson). The noisy environment of the school cafeteria might be especially challenging for this child, making it difficult for him to eat new foods or eat at all. The child may make noises or grind her teeth to block out all other sounds, making it difficult to attend to any auditory information (Flanagan). This grinding of the teeth may calm the nervous system.

AUDITORY SYSTEM

Hyper-Reactive Responses	Hypo-Reactive Responses
Reacts negatively to sounds	Appears not to hear sounds
Overwhelmed by noisy environments	Overwhelmed by noisy environment

Gustatory System (Taste)

Taste is part of the survival mechanism of the body. The gustatory system consists of four types of papillae on the body of the tongue, giving the tongue a rough surface and assisting with moving food around the mouth. One type of papillae perceives texture while the other three types contain the taste buds that detect taste, such as sweet, salty, sour, savory, and bitter tastes. All parts of the tongue are sensitive to the five different tastes (Trivedi, 2012). Taste can also alert us that something is not safe to eat and assists with discriminating food textures (Kerstein, 2008). The gustatory system is closely associated with the olfactory (smell) system. This is why food tastes differently if you have a bad cold and cannot smell the food (Ernsperger & Stegen-Hanson).

Hypo-Reactive Responses

The child who is hypo-reactive to tastes may put inedible objects with strong tastes in his mouth, such as play dough or bubbles. This child may also accept strong tastes such as hot sauce, pickles, lemons, or other spicy foods due to a need for the additional information provided by the spicier foods (Ernsperger & Stegen-Hanson). These stronger tastes help the child accept new foods as she becomes more aware of the sensation of the food in her mouth.

Hyper-Reactive Responses

The child who is hyper-reactive to tastes may resist textured foods and hot or cold temperatures. Certain textures may cause him to feel physical discomfort. This child may desire only smooth foods such as mashed potatoes and ice cream at room temperature. Also, she may accept only specific tastes, such as sweet or salty (Talk Autism, 2007).

GUSTATORY SYSTEM

Hyper-Reactive Responses	Hypo-Reactive Responses
Resists textured foods	Reduced taste discrimination
Resists hot/cold temperatures	Accepts strong tastes
Accepts only certain tastes	Eats inedible objects

Olfactory System (Smell)

Smells are registered in the nasal cavity and sent to the limbic system in the brain—the part of the brain that involves emotions and memory—which, in turn, creates reflexive-behavioral responses (Legisa, Messinger, Kermol, & Marlier, 2013). The sense of smell is present at birth and is an important source of information protecting us from something that might be dangerous to us (Kerstein), such as smoke from a fire.

The olfactory system is closely related to the gustatory, or taste, system and to emotions. For example, strong emotions are sometimes associated with certain smells because this sensation is sent to the limbic system. This is also why smells associated with an emotion are remembered (Ernsperger & Stegen-Hanson).

Hypo-Reactive Responses

The child who has hypo-reactive responses to smell may not react to potent odors, such as chlorine, as would be expected, and, therefore, not be warned about dangerous substances. (Legisa et al.). Hypo-reactive responses to smell and taste can also occur if the child is chronically congested, a fact that should be taken into consideration when working with a child who is rejecting food during the mealtime. This child will need stronger tastes in order to register information about food because the perception of taste needs a combination of information from the olfactory and gustatory systems (Ernsperger & Stegen-Hanson).

Hyper-Reactive Responses

The child who overreacts to certain smells from foods or the environment may react negatively to certain smells due to a previous emotional experience. The child may also be reacting to other smells, such as perfumes or shampoos, in the environment rather than the particular food presented to him. This oversensitivity to smells may cause the child to avoid present tasks, such as eating, because he is so overwhelmed by the smell (OCALI, 2012; Talk Autism).

OLFACTORY SYSTEM

Hyper-Reactive Responses	Hypo-Reactive Responses
Overreacts to smells from foods	Is unaware of potent odors
Avoids eating	Eats harmful substances
	Needs stronger tastes

Visual System

Approximately 75%–90% of our learning happens through our eyes. The visual system gives us information about our environment, including our position in space (Kerstein). To children with ASD, things may look uneven or blurry. According to Kaplan (2006), 18%–50% of children with ASD are unable to use both eyes together, causing them to see two images rather than one. For these reasons, children with ASD often respond in "odd" or unusual ways to what they see. For example, they may flick their fingers in front of their eyes, stare into lights, or become upset by visual stimuli such as fast-moving objects.

> **NOTE:** We are referring here to visual skills and visual processing, not visual acuity. It is important to rule out problems with visual acuity by a comprehensive eye exam.

Hypo-Reactive Responses

Children with under-reactive visual responses may not attend to visual information in their environment. As a result, they may fail to respond to food on their plate, causing a failure to eat everything on their plate (Twachtman-Reilly et al.). They may twirl objects in front of their eyes or poke fingers into the corners of the eyes while staring at a light. These are all attempts to cope with a poorly integrated visual system (Hoopes & Appelbaum, 2009).

Hyper-Reactive Responses

A child with an over-reactive visual system may shield her eyes from visual stimuli, squint, look downward, and have fleeting eye contact. This may cause her to become anxious and withdrawn, resulting in a reduction in food intake (Twachtman-Reilly et al.).

VISUAL SYSTEM

Hyper-Reactive Responses	Hypo-Reactive Responses
Covers eyes from visual stimuli	Fails to respond to visual stimuli
Decreased food intake	Does not attend to all food on plate

Behaviors associated with processing disorders in the various sensory systems are described in this chapter. This information will help parents, teachers, and caretakers understand why a child might be behaving in a certain manner during the mealtime. This will help them see that these behaviors are occurring for a reason and not just because the child is volitionally being noncompliant. This information, in turn, is essential for understanding the rationale behind a particular treatment program; with this understanding, there will be greater follow-through with the home program as well as the use of other creative means to accomplish the goals at home.

Chapter 3

Sensory Play

CHAPTER PREVIEW

Touch Activities

Vestibular Activities

Proprioceptive Activities

Olfactory Activities

The Oral Sensory Diet

Eating Utensils

Case Story

Children experience and, subsequently, accept foods through their senses. That is, they see, touch, smell, and taste foods placed in front of them. This is an important part of development in which the child encounters new foods, tastes, and textures. It should be a pleasurable experience, but unfortunately, that is often not the case for children with ASD due to their difficulties processing information through the sensory systems.

In the previous chapter, possible hypo- and hyper-reactions to information received from each sensory system are described. This chapter presents sensory activities that help the child process information and therefore assist with the acceptance of new foods by providing stimulation to touch and smell as well as the vestibular and proprioception systems. These activities can also help calm, organize, and alert the child's sensory system (Yack et al.). Sensory-based intervention assists with fine motor skills, sensory processing, regulation, and social-emotional function (Pfeiffer, Koenig, Kinnealey, Sheppard, & Henderson, 2011).

Play develops the brain. Through play, the child develops sensory input about his body and learns to adapt his responses to this input. The more varied the input, the more the child's senses are stimulated. These sensory experiences should occur in an environment where the child is encouraged and not forced to participate (Ayres). These activities can be varied to accommodate the child's interests and age level.

Touch Activities

Children with poor touch discrimination may reject new foods because of an aversion to food on their hands (Nadon et al.). They may also continue to explore through mouthing because they are not receiving enough information from the touch sensations on their hands. This may be why the child needs to have her hands cleaned as soon as she gets dirty. Play that addresses the sense of touch may help with this because it assists with the ability to tolerate a variety of sensations on their hands. The messier the better!

Tactile Bin

Fill a bin with items with different textures, such as rice, uncooked pasta, or beans for the child to explore (Kranowitz, 2006). This may also include items that the child can put to or in his mouth, such as gelatin, marshmallows, or pudding.

Finger Painting

Finger painting can be done with washable finger paints, lotion, foam soap, or foods such as pudding or yogurt. The child can paint on paper, a tray, or a Plexiglas mirror using hands or feet. Painting with foods helps the child explore foods through touch and smell at a time other than mealtime. (It is important to have a bowl of water nearby so the child can wash off his hands or feet at any time.)

Tactile Bag

Fill a bag with different cloths and textured toys that the children can feel before pulling them out of the bag.

Play Dough

Working with play dough stimulates the sense of touch. Different smells and colors can be added to homemade play dough. The child can also take part in making the play dough.

Bubble Play

If the child allows, bubbles can be blown onto the child's hands, legs, feet, or arms. This can also help with the identification of body parts, because the body parts are named each time. The child may begin to request the bubbles on a specific body part by pointing or naming. The child may even enjoy catching edible bubbles on his tongue.

Play With Lotion

This activity can begin with rubbing lotion on a baby doll and possibly naming the different parts of the doll's body while the child is rubbing on the lotion. Lotion may also be placed on a Plexiglas mirror. Here the child can be encouraged to use both hands to move up and down, side to side, or draw shapes. Faces can be drawn in the lotion to show how the child is feeling. If it is acceptable to the child, lotion can also be rubbed on parts of her body. Rubbing the feet, legs, arms, hands and face with lotion prior to meal time may help the child accept novel foods. This is part of the Oral Sensory Diet (see page 46) and can be first presented here to the child. The feet and hands can also be massaged with firm pressure without lotion (Flanagan).

Play With Utensils

A variety of spoons, forks, cups, bowls, plates, and straws can be presented to the child in a play setting. In this way, the child can get used to looking at, holding, and putting them to the lips and inside the mouth without the pressure of having something to eat or drink with them. A doll can also be offered to the child at this time to encourage additional play with the various feeding tools.

Vestibular Activities

Vestibular stimulation may help the child to sit during the meal and can help him stay organized and balanced (Yack et al.). Doing this prior to a meal or snack will give the child a greater chance for success.

Bouncing or Rocking on a Ball

Bouncing or rocking on a large ball will stimulate the vestibular system. A bouncing or jumping activity is alerting, whereas a rocking activity is calming (Yack et al.).

Movement to Music

Movement to music, either structured or unstructured, provides vestibular and auditory stimulation (Brack, 2009). Dancing to songs such as "The Hokey Pokey" gets the child moving, following directions, and predicting what comes next.

Rolling

Rolling in a barrel can be fun and give needed vestibular stimulation. The child can also be asked to follow directions, such as go fast or slow, while rolling in the barrel.

Jumping on a Trampoline

A mini trampoline can be used. The child can be encouraged to jump while listening to music, counting, reciting the alphabet, or singing a song (Kranowitz).

Proprioceptive Activities

Proprioceptive input can help the child become calm and organized by reducing overreactions to other sensations, including blocking sensations that are uncomfortable.

Movement to Music

The proprioceptive system can also be stimulated while moving to music by pairing movements that give input to the joints, such as stamping feet or marching to a song. Music that has a calming melody can help relax a child who is agitated and further assist the effects of proprioceptive input. Music that has 60 beats per minute, such as Mozart, matches the rhythm of a typical heartbeat (Brack) and can help him self-regulate. Other ways to stimulate the proprioceptive system involves adding resistance to movements, such as pushing and pulling while holding hands and singing songs like "Row, Row, Row Your Boat."

Activities on a Ball

While on their stomach over a ball, children can push forward and backward on extended arms across the floor or a mat.

Brain Gym

Brain Gym, a series of movements and activities developed by Dennison and Dennison (2015) to stimulate learning with the whole brain, are beneficial for many children prior to a meal because they stimulate organization, relaxation, and focus. More information on Brain Gym may be found at www.braingym.org.

Olfactory Activities

Smell is an important part of the eating process. A variety of scents can be offered to the child in a play environment for the purpose of calming or alerting.

Presenting Scents

When presenting different scents, begin with those that are relaxing, such as vanilla, lavender, cinnamon, or apple. These scents do not need to be placed directly under the child's nose in order for her to smell them. Present only one scent at a time so the child does not become overwhelmed and react in a negative manner (Ernsperger & Stegen-Hanson). Scents can be placed in small canisters, on a cotton ball, or in a dish of water (Yack et al.). Essential oils can also be used in a diffuser to present calming or alerting scents to the environment.

Food Jewelry

Making food jewelry is a fun activity. The child can string together pieces of fruits and vegetables and wear them on his arm or around her neck. The child can then smell each item and try to identify it (Ernsperger & Stegen-Hanson).

Scented Markers

Scented markers can be used to make placemats for mealtime. Pictures of the foods associated with each scent can be placed on the placemat. The children can talk about the different scents and the foods that are associated with them (Ernsperger & Stegen-Hanson).

The Oral Sensory Diet

Routines are an essential part of the child's treatment program. The Oral Sensory Diet is an example of a sensory-based routine that will help prepare the child's tactile system for the meal.

The goal of the Oral Sensory Diet is to help the child develop a more typical motor response of the oral structures to sensory input. Oetter, Richter, and Frick (1995) maintained that oral stimulation is important for regulating attention and mood and assists with organizing the central nervous system.

The Oral Sensory Diet is based on predictable touch input that is presented in an acceptable manner to the child. This can initially be done in a play setting, as described in the previous section. The Oral Sensory Diet is always presented at a level that the child is able to tolerate, determined by observing the child's responses prior to and during the input.

If the child is able to accept the Oral Sensory Diet without it being incorporated into play activities, it can be offered prior to a meal. The oral input will help the child interpret and discriminate the oral-tactile information received while moving the oral structures. For example, the child will feel the tongue moving to the side gums as it follows the brush from the center to the side. This movement can then be remembered and used again at a later time. For example, the child might then be able to use this lateral tongue movement to move the food to the side teeth (Flanagan).

The feet, palms, hand, tongue, lips, and face have more tactile sensory receptors than other parts of the body. Providing predictable touch stimulation to these parts of the body can have a general relaxing effect to the whole body (Escalona et al.). Developmentally, the face, lips, and tongue are the first parts of the body to be able to accurately interpret tactile information. Assisting the child with acceptance of tactile input to the oral structures may help reduce the need for excessive mouthing and eating of inedible objects.

Getting Ready

Low muscle tone can make it difficult to sit upright in a chair. The Oral Sensory Diet should be presented to the child while he is seated in a stable position, preferably at a 90° angle with feet planted firmly on the floor (Redstone, 2004). A beanbag chair can also be used, because it surrounds the child and gives information about where he is in space. This will help the child focus on the Oral Sensory Diet and not on how he is going to stay upright in the chair due to poor processing of sensory information. This is further discussed in Chapter Four.

The environment should be relatively quiet and with few visual distractions. Music that is rhythmical, one beat per second, may be played. To help the child anticipate what will happen next and thereby decrease the chance of a fight-flight-or-freeze response, a visual schedule listing the activities in the Oral Sensory Diet using picture symbols may also be presented. The child can move the picture symbols off the schedule or to another place on the schedule as each activity is completed (Lessonpix). An example of a visual schedule is found in the steps of the Oral Sensory Diet that follow.

Tools for the Oral Sensory Diet

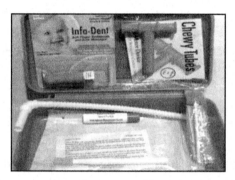

Oral sensory kit.

Through use of this kit (available for purchase at www.maureenflanagan-speech.com) and the Oral Sensory Diet, parents and professionals can help the child improve oral awareness, oral discrimination, oral stability as well as grading and separation of the oral structures. This will prepare the child for a successful mealtime. This kit can include the following items:

1. A variety of toothbrushes
2. Mini-massager
3. Flavored tongue depressors
4. Chew tubes
5. Flavored gloves
6. Variety of whistles and hum-a-zoos
7. Flavor sprays
8. Bubbles
9. Lollipops
10. Lip balm
11. Washcloths
12. Lotion
13. Powder puffs
14. Hand mitts

Steps of the Oral Sensory Diet

The Oral Sensory Diet is presented to the child in the following order:

Step 1. Rubbing With Lotion

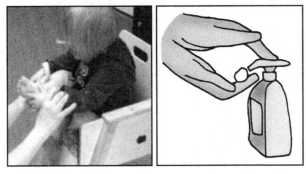

LOTION: Rubbing with lotion.

The child is encouraged to rub lotion on the areas of the body that have the most sensory touch receptors—the feet, palms, fingers, and face. This prepares the body to accept touch inside the mouth and to be in an overall relaxed state (Flanagan).

Step 2. Sensory Input to the Lips

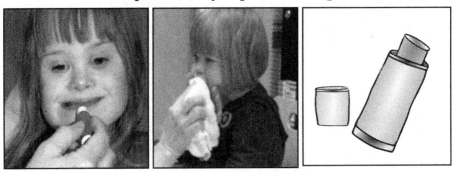

LIPS. Lip balm to the lips. Soft cloth on the lips.

It is important to focus on the lips because of all the sensory receptors located there. Flavored lip balm or a soft cloth may be applied with firm, even pressure. It is best if the child can apply the input on her own. If this is not possible, it is essential to tell the child that you will be touching her lips. The input to the lips helps with oral awareness and oral discrimination (Flanagan). The schedule assists the child in knowing what to expect next.

Step 3. Up/Down Chewing Movements

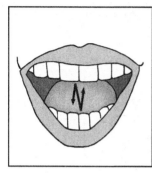

CHEWING. Chewing on a chew tube.

The chew tube helps develop jaw stability, which is needed for separate and graded movements of the tongue and lips (www.chewytubes.com). This means that the tongue and lips can move separately with control from the lower jaw and each other. Encourage the child to use up/down chewing movements on the chew tube, which is placed on the side teeth. The chewing should be rhythmical, 10–30 times on each side. Counting or clapping out loud can help the child understand how many times to chew on each side. It is important to make sure the child's lower jaw is moving up and down and not side-to-side or forward, because moving the lower jaw side to side or forward and backward does not help to develop jaw stability.

This is also a time to work on controlling the size of the mouth opening while chewing on the chew tube. This is called grading of jaw movements. This may be done by verbally asking the child to "make a small mouth" or physically assisting the child with jaw control (Flanagan). Jaw control is accomplished by placing a hand or finger under the child's chin with a thumb under the lower lip to facilitate a smaller mouth opening (Redstone).

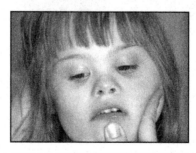

Jaw control.

Step 4. Separate Tongue Movement

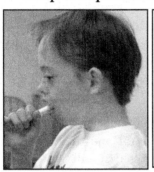 

TONGUE BRUSH. Firm input onto the tongue.

The Nuk Brush or ARK Probe are used to increase oral awareness, improve oral discrimination, and modify oral sensitivity (www.arktherapeutic.com, www.beyondplay.com). The child is asked to push down on the tongue while the tongue is inside the mouth. This is working on separation of lower jaw movement from tongue movement. If there is no separation of tongue movement from jaw movement, the child will have difficulty keeping the tongue in the mouth with the mouth opening.

Continue working on the child's ability to control the size of the mouth opening. This may be done again with jaw control and the verbal prompt, "use a small mouth." The child or adult pushes down on the tongue 10 to 30 times (Flanagan). This will increase oral awareness and oral discrimination and regulate the sensitivity of the body of the tongue while the tongue is inside of the mouth (Clark, 2006; Lazarus, 2006; Sheppard, 2006). Next, the child or you brush both sides of the tongue. This facilitates tongue movement toward the side teeth, which will help lateral tongue movement while chewing. This is necessary for moving food and keeping food on the biting edges of the teeth. Following this, ask the child to push down on the tip of the tongue and then touch the top of the mouth. Typically, the tongue follows the tactile stimulation and moves to the top of the mouth. This encourages separate tongue movement and assists with regulating oral sensitivity. If the child cannot do this himself, then you can assist with this.

Other exercises may be used to help strengthen the tongue involving movement against resistance, called isometric exercises (strength training exercises) (Anderson, 2001). They are effective for improving tongue strength, coordinated tongue movements, swallow function, and muscle skills (Bathel, 2006).

The parent, teacher, or therapist holds the Nuk Brush or ARK Probe on the front of the child's tongue while the tongue is inside the mouth. The child is instructed to push up against this resistance to the top of the mouth five to ten times. The same exercise may also be done with the sides and tip of the tongue.

Also part of the sensory environment are the eating utensils used during the meal. Because children with ASD may have difficulty using typical utensils, it is important to select ones that will make it easier for them to eat their snack or meal.

Eating Utensils

A variety of utensils may assist with mealtime. It is important to expose children with ASD to a variety of utensils, because many of them want to use the same cup, spoon, or plate during all meals. Modeling by an adult or peer may help (Bruns & Thompson). It is essential to choose utensils of the appropriate size for the child. For example, a large dinner plate may be overwhelming for a young child. The following are examples of utensils that can be used with the child. This is a sample of what is available and is not meant to be an endorsement of any particular product.

Spoons

These maroon spoons have a shallow bowl and help the child clean the spoon as well as control the amount of food he puts into his mouth. When picking a spoon, it is important to consider the amount of food the spoon can hold and the ability to get lip closure on the spoon (www.beyondplay.com).

Scoop Bowls

Scoop Bowls have a unique shape that helps with scooping the food onto the spoon (www.beyondplay.com).

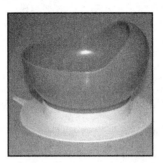

Scoop Plates

Scoop Plates have a lip that helps keep the food on the plate and helps the child maneuver it onto the spoon or fork (www.beyondplay.com).

Cut-Out Cups

Cut-Out Cups help the child drink the liquid at the bottom of the cup without having to tip her head back (www.beyondplay.com).

Straw Bear

The Straw Bear makes it easier for the child to drink from a straw. The liquid in the honey bear can be squeezed up into the straw. The plastic straw holds its shape while the child drinks from the straw (www.beyondplay.com).

Case Story

John has a diagnosis of ASD. He sits for short periods of time but prefers to spin, jump, and fall onto the floor. John's diet consists of dried fruit, yogurt, pudding, chicken nuggets, and bananas. He declines new foods and often does not want to brush his teeth or wash his hair. He likes to take off his shoes, socks, pants, and shirt, and it is often a struggle to put them back on again.

John frequently paces back and forth and crashes into the walls due to under-reactive vestibular and proprioceptive systems that make it difficult for him to sit still for long periods of time. He has difficulty processing tactile input as seen through his need to take off his clothes, shoes, and socks and his attempts to evade teeth brushing and hair washing. This affects his diet, which is extremely limited.

John interacts with sensory play activities prior to having a new food introduced to him. He enjoys marching and moving to the rhythm of the music and playing drums to the beat. Touch activities are also available for him. He likes to paint with washable paints or pudding, provided there is a way to quickly clean his hands.

John enjoys peppermint, lavender, and lemon scents on a cotton ball but prefers the smell of peppermint. It helps him to smell this prior to the Oral Sensory Diet. After this alerting activity, he rubs lotion on his feet, legs, hands, arms, and face and rubs his lips with a washcloth. He prefers this to lip balms. He finishes with the chew tube and arc probe for a count of 20 or the duration of singing a short song.

Consistent presentation of these activities prior to the introduction of new foods helps John sit at a table, facilitates a general, more relaxed state, and increases his tolerance for textures and tastes.

The child with ASD may resist trying something new or different. She needs to be motivated to do this. Play may be the way to motivate her to try a new activity that will help her regulate her sensory system. The activities presented in this chapter are meant to do just that. They give the child a reason to try them: because they are fun!

The Oral Sensory Diet and kit are meant to be used and presented to the child in a predictable, fun manner. This will help the child accept the sensory input, develop body awareness, and then, hopefully, produce the appropriate movements while eating and drinking. The regularity and predictability of the Oral Sensory Diet is meant to satisfy the child's need to experience an activity or sensation a few times before it registers as being enjoyable (Ayres).

Chapter 4

The Environment

Just as the presentation of the Oral Sensory Diet needs to be predictable and structured, so does the child's environment in order to ensure a successful session. Children with a diagnosis of ASD often have difficulty with joint attention, the shared attention of an object or event with another person (Yack et al.). This may make it challenging for them to connect and interact with their environment, causing them to become anxious and confused, and may lead to aversive and aggressive behaviors. Many children also have difficulty with multiple sensory stimuli, which may cause them to attend to only part of a complex direction or cue, including those that are not important to the total picture. For example, because of loud background music, the child may only attend to the music and not to your voice.

Competing sensory stimuli may produce negative behaviors because the child becomes overwhelmed and unable to process any of the information. For example, if the child eats in a room where there are people moving past the child, loud music playing, and brightly colored pictures on the wall, the child may be unable to focus on his food. Therefore, it is important to structure the environment so children can comprehend the verbal and nonverbal cues, thus increasing the ability to predict what may happen next.

The following sections describe the best physical and sensory environments for feeding.

Physical Environment

The physical area where new foods or foods that are not tolerated are presented to the child must be an organized space away from the table where family meals take place or the school cafeteria. Otherwise, the social demands of these environments may cause added stress, making it difficult for the child to focus on the challenge of eating a new food (Nadon et al.). A quiet part of the home or classroom away from areas of movement helps eliminate accidental touching by others. The separate space helps the child predict what is going to occur during the snack or meal. Furthermore, use of items that could distract the child, such as toys or videos, should be limited. Once food is accepted in this space, the child may then be brought to the family table or the cafeteria.

Seating Options

The child should be in a stable sitting position, as close to 90° as possible, with feet firmly on the floor or foot rest. The table should match the height of the chair so that the child is in a comfortable position (Twachtman-Reilly et al.), sitting upright, with her body in the middle. Weighted vests, weighted pillows, and weighted blankets may help the child maintain a stable sitting position while eating her meal (Yack et al.). Another option is a beanbag chair, which offers a large area of support (Flanagan) by "surrounding" the child's body.

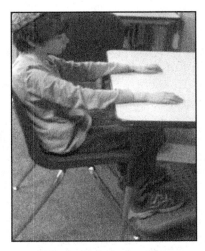

Sitting with feet supported.

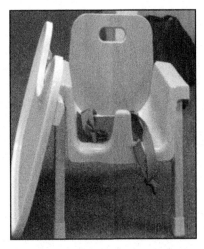

Chair with extra supports.

Beanbag chair.

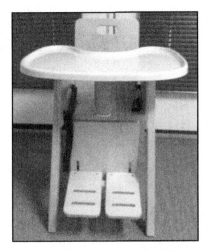

Chair with removable tray, adjustable feet support, and pelvis support.

Visual Schedules

Visual cues are critical for children with ASD because this information is concrete and not fleeting like auditory information. Visual stimuli such as pictures, symbols, or printed words are permanent, unlike the spoken word. Therefore, visual cues make it easier to process the information, make the environment more predictable, and assist with transitions between activities. In this section we look at some examples of visual supports, including a first-then board, a transition board, and a visual schedule for the school day or a particular activity.

Visual schedules are used in a variety of situations to adapt the environment for children with ASD (Cafiero, 2005). They can be made with picture communication symbols, photos, line drawings, or the written word and represent specific activities or tasks that will be presented to the child. The visual schedules can be used to tell what will happen, what is happening now, and what has been completed. A symbol can be moved from a strip on the left side of the board (what will happen) to a center strip (what is happening) to a right strip (what has finished happening). The symbol can also be removed to a pocket to indicate that the task or activity is done (Cafiero).

By their nature, visual schedules assist with cooperation during an activity or mealtime because they enable the child to better predict, sequence, and comprehend what is happening and will happen during the session or activity. Ultimately, this reduces anxiety and stress and therefore often reduces challenging behaviors.

A visual schedule can be used to list when mealtime will occur during the daily activities. During the meal, the visual schedule can also let the child know when the meal will be over. Many children with ASD have difficulty judging when mealtime is over, which may cause them to over- or under-eat (Twachtman-Reilly et al.). The schedule presents them with the sequence of foods to be offered. The child can also see when he will need to eat a new or non-preferred food and when he will receive a preferred food.

A first-then board can also be used to show the sequence of presentation of preferred food versus non-preferred food. Using preferred foods as a reinforcer can increase the consumption of new foods (Galle, 2010). It is important to include foods on the schedule that the child accepts. An example of a first-then board and a snacktime schedule are shown in Figures 4.1 and 4.2, respectively.

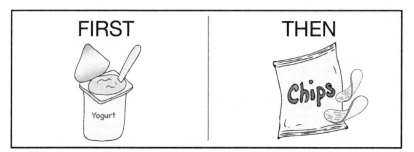

Figure 4.1. First-then board.

Figure 4.2. Visual schedule.
Symbols courtesy of Lessonpix.

Finally, a timer—also a visual symbol—may help create predictability by letting the child know how long the mealtime will be and when it will be over (Bodison et al.).

Sensory Environment

A well-functioning sensory system enables us to filter out information that is not relevant and respond to information that is important amid the multitude of sensory information that is constantly bombarding us (Twachtman-Reilly et al.). Due to difficulty doing just this, a child with ASD can become easily overwhelmed by the world around her. Thus, when the child's sensory system is overloaded, it interferes with his ability to cope and function (Sears, 2010), triggering emotions and behaviors that are difficult for him to control (Kerstein). The next sections discuss how auditory and visual stimulation can affect the feeding sensory environment. These two sensory channels are targeted because regulation of these stimuli will greatly assist with decreasing multiple cues and competing sensory stimuli that can interfere with the mealtime as discussed in the chapter introduction.

Auditory Stimulation

Children with ASD frequently have difficulty filtering out background noise, making it hard to attend to important information (Nadon et al.). In addition, they may be hypersensitive to auditory information, which can be physically painful, causing the child to cover her ears or make noises to block out the input (Hoekman). Not surprisingly, an environment such as the school cafeteria can be overwhelming and make it difficult for her to focus on the foods to be eaten due to multiple sensory experiences, including the noise from conversation, the scraping of trays on the tables, and the humming of fluorescent lights.

The language presented to the child during the meal also is part of the sensory environment and therefore a component of the sensory information the child needs to process. Language should be simple, using grammatically correct sentences. A slow rate of speech with pauses after each sentence helps with auditory processing of the information presented. Furthermore, using the word "Listen" prior to communicating the actual message alerts the child that essential information is coming. Also, starting the session with the same phrase, such as "It is time to eat," will help the child know what to expect—in this case, that you will be working on his eating skills (Flanagan).

If the child is eating in a noisy environment like a school cafeteria, some relatively simple accommodations may be made to support her. For example, the child could go early and begin to eat prior to the other students arriving; the time spent in the cafeteria could be decreased; and a smaller table could be set up for the child with one or two other students away from the larger tables. This would decrease the amount of traffic walking by the table and anyone accidentally touching the child with ASD. The child could wear noise reduction-headphones or listen to music through stereo head-phones to help her tolerate background noise (Yack et al.). Finally, if these accommodations are not working, the child could be allowed to eat in the classroom or another environment that is less stimulating.

Brian, a 10-year-old boy with ASD, was a student in a special education pro-gram that was housed in a private school. Brian was mainstreamed for specials and some classes. The cafeteria was challenging for him due to the noise level and the movement of students walking past his seat at the lunch table. He also had difficulty conversing with the students from his general education class-room who sat with him at lunch. As a result, he often sat without speaking and only ate snack foods from his lunch box.

To get Brian more involved with his classmates and eating a proper lunch, the speech-language pathologist and the psychologist at the school developed a "Lunch Bunch" program for Brian to take place in the psychologist's office with two other students from Brian's classroom. The students, who were hand selected by the psychologist, changed on a weekly basis. Eight students were selected for the program and each group committed to 1 week per month. The students received service hours for helping with the Lunch Bunch program.

Brian began to eat his lunch in this quiet environment and converse in the structured group, which was led by the speech-language pathologist or the psychologist. The goal was to move the group to a small table in the cafeteria 1 day each week. This was attempted toward the end of the school year, but the cafeteria was still too difficult for Brian. The program was continued for the rest of the school year in the quiet environment.

Visual Stimulation

Many children with ASD have a poorly developed and integrated visual system that results in poor eye contact, a lack of depth perception, difficulty visually attending to sounds or voices and focusing on fast-moving objects or people. As a result, these children may struggle to interpret and accurately process what they see in their environment (Hoopes & Applebaum, 2009). This is why visual supports are important. A visual schedule helps to add order and consistency to an environment that otherwise causes confusion.

Because of the increased effort needed to process visual information, environmental factors such as lighting can affect the child's overall performance during the mealtime. Thus, changing the lighting in the room may help the child's ability to focus on the meal. For example, a dimmer switch can help set the lights at the right level for each child. If lights cannot be dimmed, sunglasses or a visor may help the child tolerate the bright lights.

Other factors that can affect the child's visual system are patterns on the table or plate. The child may have difficulty finding the food against a visual pattern. She may also become distracted from eating by these patterns and place her face close to the plate to block out the extra input (Yack et al.). Decreasing the extra visual input will assist with the child's ability to focus on the food on the plate. One solution would be to use a plate with a solid color rather than a pattern.

> *Arthur, a 7-year-old boy with ASD, was a student in a special education program that was housed in a private school. He stayed in his regular second-grade classroom during the school day with support from a shadow support assistant. Arthur had difficulty with bright lights and did not want to eat in the school cafeteria with his classmates. He frequently sat at the lunch table with his head down on the table. This interfered with him eating his lunch and interacting with his classmates.*
>
> *Because of his sensitivity to lights, Arthur always carried sunglasses and a baseball cap with him to wear outside at recess. After observing Arthur's challenges in the cafeteria, he was allowed to do the same during lunch. The students were used to him wearing these at recess, so it was not considered unusual for him to wear them in the cafeteria. This enabled Arthur to eat his lunch and occasionally interact with his classmates at the lunch table.*

The support provided by a structured environment will enable children with ASD to focus on the task of eating and drinking. Supports are often simple and easy to arrange, such as providing a stable seating position or changing the plate so it does not have a pattern on it. By observing the child and consulting with those working with the child, a supportive physical and sensory environment can be developed for the child.

Chapter 5

Assessment

James, a 2 ½-year-old boy with ASD, had a very limited diet. He ate only one kind of macaroni and cheese and chicken nuggets, refusing any variation in the brand or appearance of these foods. He also ate raw broccoli but refused it if it was cooked. He only ate these foods at home. He ate McDonald's French fries but only while riding in the car. Any attempt to present these foods in other locations met with refusals and tantrums.

    In spite of weekly treatment for feeding skills by a trained professional, his feeding behaviors remain the same. However, a full assessment has never been performed of James' feeding and medical history, a food journal has never been compiled, nor has James' oral structures been observed at rest and during the feeding process.

A feeding assessment is recommended when there are concerns about the child's: a) weight and height; b) food refusal or extreme selectivity with food choices; c) oral movements while eating; and d) medical and behavioral issues that may affect the feeding process (Galle). Referrals for a feeding assessment may come from a variety of sources, such as the pediatrician, speech-language pathologist (SLP), occupational therapist (OT), or classroom teacher.

The assessment should be conducted by a professional trained in observing movement patterns and behaviors during the feeding process. Typically, this is an SLP or an OT. The evaluation should take place in a setting that allows the person doing the assessment to observe the child eating and drinking. While this may vary, because some children only eat in one particular location, the preferred location is one where there are minimal distractions.

This chapter describes what is needed to assess the child's dietary intake, the tastes and textures of foods eaten by the child, the level of development of food intake and oral movement patterns, the presence of any atypical patterns of movement, and the environmental needs of the individual child as well as any medical, physical, or behavioral issues. A feeding problem may have begun as a medical issue but became a behavioral problem after the medical issue was resolved with the child. For example, at a younger age, the child may have suffered from gastroesophageal reflux, a disease whereby the stomach acid comes back into the esophagus and sometimes reaches the back of the throat. Understandably, this makes the feeding experience unpleasant. The emotional response to such an experience may remain for the child even after the medical problem has resolved.

Developmental History

The developmental history consists of the child's feeding history and medical history. This information is compiled through a parent/caretaker interview. Feeding and medical questionnaires are used to guide the interview process, as illustrated in the following.

Parent/Caretaker Interview

When taking a child's feeding history, information is collected from the child's parents or primary caretaker about the child's ability to easily and rhythmically nurse or drink formula from a bottle and about the child's feeding milestones. Examples of milestones include age and ability to accept: a) solid foods from a spoon; b) a cup; c) textured food; and d) table foods. The guideline for the age and ease with which the child is able to move through these milestones is based on typical development (see Chapter Two). A comparison to typical development will reveal whether or not the skills observed in the child are part of typical development, delayed movement patterns, primitive movement patterns, or atypical movement patterns.

The child's medical history should also be collected at this time. As stated earlier, many children with a diagnosis of ASD have a history of gastroesophageal reflux or slow gastric emptying (Bruns & Thompson), whereby the stomach contents move into the esophagus due to a relaxing of the sphincter muscle between the stomach and the esophagus. This can cause a variety of symptoms, including heartburn, nausea, coughing, and vomiting (Ernsperger & Stegel-Hanson). Other medical issues include inflammatory bowel disease such as enterocolitis, esophagitis, gastritis (Wheeler, 2004), food allergies, and constipation or diarrhea. These gastrointestinal issues may cause general difficulty accepting foods due to the child's inability to identify the source of the problem while attempting to prevent distress during mealtimes (Twachtman-Reilly et al.). Procedures such as a barium swallow, gastric emptying study, allergy testing, or a gastrointestinal probe may be required prior to the initiation of treatment for a feeding disorder (Galle).

Children with ASD often have difficulty communicating their discomfort. Therefore, it is essential to know about these issues through the parent or caretaker reports. Some sample questions about feeding development and medical history are listed in Figures 5.1 and 5.2, respectively (blank forms are also provided in the Appendix).

Questions About Feeding Development

1. Did you breastfeed your child right after birth?
   A. How long did it take your child to breastfeed?
   B. Until what age did your child breastfeed?
   C. Was there a difficulty that caused you to bottle feed?

2. If bottle fed, what type of nipple was used with your child?
   A. How long did it take for your child to complete an 8-ounce bottle?
   B. What age did you stop breastfeeding or bottle feeding?

3. At what age did your child:
   A. Accept solid food from a spoon?
   • What type of food was first accepted by your child?
   • What type of spoon was used?
   • Does your child feed him-/herself with a spoon?

   B. Accept textured food from a spoon?
   • What type of textured food is accepted by spoon (mashed lumpy, ground food)?

   C. Eat table foods?
   • What type of food did he/she first accept?
   • What type of food does he/she accept now?
   • Did he/she refuse any type of table food?

   D. Finger feed table foods?
   • What type of food did he/she first accept? (crunchy, soft, or hard)
   • What type of food does he/she accept now?
   • Did he/she refuse any or all types of finger food?
   • Does your child chew finger foods?
   • Does your child move foods side to side in the mouth?
   • How long is a typical mealtime?

Figure 5.1. Feeding development questionnaire.
Source: Bruns & Thompson, 2011. Used with permission.

Questions About Feeding Development *(cont.)*

E. Drink from a cup (assisted and unassisted)?
- What liquids did he/she first accept? (water, juices, thickened drinks)
- What liquids does he/she accept now?
- What type of cup does he/she use?

F. Drink from a straw?

G. Become aware of food on his/her face?
- Does your child continue to be a messy eater?
- Does food fall out of his/her mouth?
- Does he/she store food in the cheeks?

H. Begin to feed him/herself?
- At what age did your child feed him/herself?
- How long does it take for your child to feed him/herself?
- What utensils can your child use?

I. Begin and stop exploring objects by mouth?
- Does your child put inedible objects in his/her mouth?

J. Begin and stop drooling?
- Does your child drool only at specific times?

4. **Have there been concerns about your child's overall developmental growth?**

5. **Does your child accept new foods?** Does he/she have a preference for a certain food group?

6. **How many meals/snacks does your child eat in 1 day?** Does your child sit at a table for meals?

7. **What is your child's school history?**

Figure 5.1. Feeding development questionnaire (*cont.*)

Figure 5.2 lists sample questions about medical history that are helpful to ask during the parent interview.

Questions About Medical History

1. **Does your child have food allergies?**
   A. Is your child on a special diet?
   B. Has your child had a reaction to any foods?

2. **Has your child had a history of choking or gagging on food?**
   A. Has there been difficulty swallowing any foods or liquids?
   B. Has your child ever needed to receive tube feedings? (nasogastric or gastrostomy tube)
   C. Has food ever come out of your child's nose?

3. **Is your child a picky eater?**

4. **Does your child have any gastrointestinal problems such as reflux, diarrhea, or constipation?**

5. **Is your child taking any medications?** Are there any known side effects for the medications?

6. **Does your child grind his/her teeth?**

7. **Has your child been hospitalized since birth?**

8. **Has your child been hospitalized for any surgery?**

9. **Is your child's height and weight within the normal range for his/her age?** Do you have any concerns about height and weight?

10. **What physicians are currently taking care of your child?** Does your child have a medical diagnosis?

11. **What therapists are currently working with your child?** Has there been any prior testing for speech/language skills and feeding skills?

Figure 5.2. Medical history questionnaire.

Source: Bruns & Thompson, 2011. Used with permission.

After compiling information on the child's feeding and medical history, the parents or primary caretakers as well as professionals working with the child are asked by the professional conducting the assessment to develop a food journal.

Food Journal

The food journal consists of a compilation of the foods currently eaten and accepted by the child over a short time period in a variety of environments. The parents complete a food journal for meals consumed at home and while out in the community. In addition, the teacher compiles a food journal for foods eaten in the classroom and the cafeteria and the SLP and/or OT record foods eaten during the therapy sessions (Bruns & Thompson). An example of a food journal for home on Saturday might look like this:

Breakfast: 5 spoonfuls applesauce, 3 oz. water

Lunch: 10 barbecued chips, 3 oz. water, 6 spoonfuls strawberry yogurt

Snack: 8 oz. vanilla PediaSure (nutritional supplement), 10 barbecued chips

Dinner: 8 spoonfuls warm tomato soup, 4 oz. PediaSure

As illustrated, the food journal provides information about the type, taste, temperature, texture, and amount of foods typically eaten by the child during all meals and snacks. It also tells how the child is eating in different environments and with different individuals. The parents and caretakers may also be observed with the child to determine if any problem behaviors are being reinforced during the meal (Galle); for example, a caretaker may be giving the child a lot of attention during avoidance behaviors, such as screaming and throwing food, which may be supporting these behaviors. Any kind of attention may be reinforcing, even saying "no."

Feeding Assessment

The third part of the assessment involves the SLP or OT observing the child while eating a snack or meal. It is important to directly observe the child while eating, along with what is reported in the feeding history and food journal.

Observation of the Oral Structures at Rest

The child's oral structures are observed at rest by the SLP or OT to determine symmetry, muscle tone, and structure. This should take place in a quiet setting where the child feels comfortable (see Chapter Four). In the following section, the typical appearance of the oral structures is described in detail. It is important to know what the typical appearance of the oral structures is so that any deviations can be easily noted by the examiner.

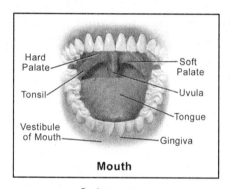

Oral structures.
Image credit: Blausen, 2014

Lips: Both sides of the upper and lower lips should be symmetrical. If the child is 4 months or older, there should be lip closure and nasal breathing at rest.

Gums: The gums should be balanced with an even contour.

Tongue: The tongue should have a thin, bowl-shaped configuration with both sides of the tongue similar in appearance. In the newborn, there is more of a cupped tongue configuration with a groove down the middle to assist with the flow of liquids.

Hard Palate: The hard palate is a horizontal plate of bone that separates the nose from the mouth and goes from one side of the upper teeth to the other. It is light pink in color with ridges in the front of the palate. These ridges help to break down the food to assist with swallowing. There is also a suture or bony ridge running down the middle of the palate. The distance and shape of the hard palate on either side of this bony ridge to the side teeth should be the same on both sides of the mouth. The hard palate should not have a high, narrow contour. It should be more dome shaped.

Soft Palate: The soft palate is connected to the end of the hard palate and is made of soft tissue. It prevents food from entering the nose during swallowing. At the end of the soft palate is a structure called the uvula. The uvula is a fleshy lobe that hangs down off of the soft palate.

Upper Jaw: The upper jaw, or maxilla, consists of two bones that are fused together at the middle of the hard palate. A portion of the hard palate, this bone holds the upper teeth, separates the nose from the mouth, and forms the floor of the bone that holds the eyes. The upper jaw should be slightly larger than the lower jaw so that the teeth of the upper jaw fit over the teeth of the lower jaw.

Lower Jaw: The lower jaw, or mandible, is a U-shaped bone that stretches from one ear to the other. It attaches to each side of the skull. The body of the lower jaw holds the lower teeth. The lower jaw should be symmetrical at the midline of the mouth.

Cheeks: The cheeks are formed by the paired zygomatic bone. This bone attaches to the upper jaw and other bones of the skull. Both cheekbones should be symmetrical.

Teeth: There are 32 permanent teeth housed in the upper and lower jaws. Most children have all of their permanent teeth by 13 years of age. The teeth of the upper jaw typically extend over the teeth of the lower jaw (Travis, 1971). There are 20 primary or baby teeth, 10 on the upper jaw and 10 on the lower jaw. Children begin to lose their primary teeth between ages 6 and 7 years (WebMD, 2012).

The Oral Structures/Movement Worksheet (see Figure 5.3; a blank copy is also provided in the Appendix) may be used to detail the child's movement patterns and subsequently serve as a baseline of skills. It can also chart progress with the child's movements at rest, during simple movements, and while eating a meal or snack. Following these observations, a decision can be made as to whether the child's movement patterns can be classified as being: a) within typical limits; b) reflexive or primitive; c) delayed; or d) atypical (revised from Flanagan). These movement patterns are described in Chapter Two. The child's developmental level for eating skills and food textures will become evident following the completion of the feeding history, food journal, and the Oral Structures/Movement Worksheet by the SLP or OT. Also identified is the best environment to begin treatment with the child based on the information compiled about the child through developmental history, food journal, and direct observation.

Case Story

*RT, a 5-year-old boy with ASD, was evaluated for a feeding disorder. A devel-
opmental feeding questionnaire was used to obtain information from his parents about his feeding history. The parents reported that breastfeeding had
been difficult for RT due to a minimal ability to maintain a suck-swallow on
the breast. He had been bottle fed a soy-based formula with a longer nipple
until 2 years of age. It had typically taken 30 minutes for him to finish a 4-oz
bottle. He had turned down rice cereal from a spoon at 5 months of age. The
pediatrician had recommended putting rice cereal in the bottle, which RT had
accepted.*

*Thin puréed pears were presented to RT at 6 months of age from an
infant-sized spoon. He frequently pushed this out of his mouth with forward/
backward tongue movement. It took 15–20 minutes to feed him 1 tbsp. of food.
Carrots, bananas, apples, and plums were also presented to RT from an infant-
sized spoon between 6 and 8 months. It also took 15–20 minutes for him to
finish 1 tbsp. of these foods. At 8 months of age, rice cereal was added to the
thin purée but RT declined it. At 9 months of age, RT accepted stage 2 baby
foods. Mashed bananas were unsuccessfully attempted at 10 months of age;
RT gagged when the bananas were placed in his mouth with the spoon, and
he spit them out. He also became upset when food got on his hands and face
and wanted to be immediately cleaned up. At 18 months of age, he began to
feed himself from a small, infant-sized spoon. He continues to feed himself thin
puréed food from a spoon.*

*Formula was unsuccessfully presented to RT from a cup at 10 months of
age. He finally accepted a cup with handles at 2 years of age. He continues to
drink from this cup. At 2 years of age, RT fed himself barbecue potato chips.
He continues to only eat the same brand of barbecue potato chips and regular
potato chips. At this time, 5 years of age, RT has been reported to frequently
put toys, other inedible objects, and lotion in his mouth. However, he did not
explore toys orally or put hands to mouth at the appropriate developmental
age of 4–6 months.*

*After completing the medical questionnaire, it was revealed that RT had a
history of reflux but no longer takes medication for it. He is frequently consti-
pated and takes supplements to alleviate this problem.*

The food journal was completed for one week for all of RT's meals and snacks. He fed himself thin, puréed foods at room temperature for breakfast, lunch, and dinner. These had to be the same brand of jarred baby food. Any attempt to offer a different brand was not met with success. He always smelled his food prior to eating it. These behaviors were noted both in the home and school environments. In school, RT ate in the kindergarten classroom with six other classmates. All of his food and drink were sent from home. He fed himself with a spoon and bowl also sent from home and drank his protein shake from his preferred cup with handles. He did best when allowed to sit at a table by himself away from the group. During the scheduled snack time, he ate his barbecued potato chips sitting at a table with his classmates. These chips were his preferred food. He ate the chips quickly, stuffing a large amount into his mouth at one time. Many of the chips fell out of his mouth onto the table and floor. RT was aware of this and ate the remaining chips off of the table and floor. At home, RT ate all his meals at the kitchen table. He frequently got up after he finished eating even though the rest of the family was still eating at the table. He did allow his face to be wiped after each meal. This was also reported at school. RT did not like to have his face wiped but did tolerate it for a short period.

In RT's case, the feeding behaviors reported during the feeding history or food journal that give cause for concern include difficulty accepting textured foods, overreactions to smells or sounds in the mealtime environment, stuffing food in the mouth, storing food in the cheeks, spitting out food, losing food out of the mouth while eating, and gagging during the presentation of foods. Other behaviors that give cause for concern include continuing to mouth objects past 2 years of age, difficulty using utensils, and lack of awareness of food around and on the mouth (Bodison et al.).

The oral structures were observed during simple movements and are noted in Figure 5.3. There was symmetry in the movements of the oral structures. This means that both sides of the oral structures moved the same amount. The upper and lower lips were tight as seen through the pursed and thin lips during movement. The wide mouth openings with full extension of the lower jaw indicated poor jaw stability. RT was unable to produce isolated movement of the cheeks, which could indicate tightness of the muscles of the lower jaw. The tongue remained pulled far back in the mouth during all attempts to produce movement of the tongue. This tongue position and posture showed tension of all muscles of the tongue.

Also noted was a lack of separation of lip and tongue movements from lower jaw movement. The muscles of the face, lips, and tongue had limited range of movement. RT also has a diagnosis of low muscle tone.

Oral hypersensitivity was noted due to the hyperactive gag reflex stimulated by touch to the front of the tongue and the refusal to eat textured foods. RT continues to be a mouth breather, which is unusual for someone his age.

Delayed and atypical movement patterns were observed while RT was eating from a spoon, drinking from a cup, and chewing crunchy solids. The delayed movement patterns included:

- biting on the cup edge while drinking from the cup,
- liquid loss while drinking,
- wide mouth opening for the cup and spoon, and
- lack of upper lip movement on the cup and spoon.

These are all movements seen in typical development but at a younger age. The atypical movement patterns noted included:

- the tongue held back in the mouth with a thick, bunched tongue posture;
- the lack of lateral tongue movement while chewing;
- the swallowing of the thin puree and crunchy solid with forward/backward tongue movements and a bunched tongue; the gulping of the liquid with only two to three sip/swallows at a time;
- the tight, thin lips with reduced range of motion of the upper/lower lips;
- the chewing of only crunchy solids;
- the lack of awareness of food loss and food around the mouth; and
- the refusal of hot or cold food temperatures.

These behaviors and movement patterns would not be observed in the typical population.

Questions About Oral Structures/Movement

Name: RT	Birthday: 5/7/2010
Age: 5 years, 2 months	Date: 7/15/2015
Diagnosis: Autism spectrum disorder	

1. Oral Structures: Appearance at Rest

1. Lips:

   Pulling back of upper and lower lips. Meet in a tight line at midline.

2. Gums:

   Pink, smooth and symmetrical.

3. Tongue:

   Tongue pulled back into mouth. Thick and bunched.

4. Cheeks:

   Similar in size and shape.

5. Upper Jaw:

   Teeth of upper jaw slightly forward of lower jaw.

6. Lower Jaw:

   Symmetrical and held in a midline position at rest.

7. Hard Palate:

   Pink, high and narrow.

8. Soft Palate:

   Pink with uvula held in midline. Adequate length.

9. Teeth:

   Two lower, first molars have been capped due to decay. Does not have any secondary teeth.

Figure 5.3. Oral structures/movement worksheet completed for RT.
Source: Revised from Flanagan, 2008. Used with permission.

2. Oral Structures During Movement: I: (imitation) S: (spontaneous)
(Note asymmetries, movement patterns, and ability to produce separate movements)

A. Lower Jaw/Upper Jaw
   1. Open mouth:
     (S), Wide mouth opening with wide eye opening upon request. Tongue was pulled back in his mouth.

   2. Smile:
     (I), Both sides of mouth moved in symmetry, lower jaw stayed in midline. Tight smile.

   3. Open/close mouth:
     (I), Full extension of lower jaw with tongue pulled back in mouth.

B. Lips
   4. Pucker:
     (I), Lips rounded with symmetry, tension in lips, more pursing of the lips.

   5. Blow:
     (S), Lips were tightly rounded while blowing.

   6. Hum:
     (I), Tight lip closure at midline, one hum at a time.

   7. Oo-ee:
     (I), Slow movements while rounding and retracting the lips.

   8. Lip smack:
     (I), Wide movements of lower jaw.

C. Cheeks
   9. Puff out cheeks:
     Could not imitate.

Figure 5.3. Oral structures/movement worksheet completed for RT (*cont.*)
Source: Revised from Flanagan, 2008. Used with permission.

2. Oral Structures During Movement: I: (imitation) S: (spontaneous) (cont.)

D. Tongue

10. Tongue out (with mouth open):
(I), Wide mouth opening with tongue pulled back in mouth.

11. Tongue out/in (with mouth open):
Mouth opened and closed with tongue back in mouth. Unable to imitate.

12. Tongue tip up inside of mouth:
Unable to imitate.

13. Tongue tip to upper lip:
(I), Lower jaw moved forward and attempted to move tongue forward by biting on tongue.

14. Tongue tip down inside of mouth:
Unable to imitate.

15. Tongue tip to chin:
(I), Wide jaw with tongue moving to lower lip.

16. Tongue side to side to mouth corners:
Unable to imitate.

17. Tongue side to side to lower teeth:
Unable to imitate.

18. Tongue side to side to cheeks:
Unable to imitate.

19. Tongue side to side to upper teeth:
Unable to imitate.

20. Tongue click:
Wide open closing of the lower jaw/mouth, No separate movement of tongue. Unable to imitate

Figure 5.3. Oral structures/movement worksheet completed for RT (*cont.*)
Source: Revised from Flanagan, 2008. Used with permission.

3. Oral and Postural Muscle Tone

A. Facial tone:
Tight, deep lines alongside nose to upper lip. Difficult to pull both cheeks forward to mouth corners. Upper and lower lips do not move downward or upward with full range.

B. Lingual tone:
Not able to palpate the tongue due to pulling back into the mouth. Thick and bunched in appearance.

C. Body tone:
Diagnosed with hypotonia.

4. Breathing

A. Oral breather:
Primarily a mouth breather.

B. Nasal breather:
Can close mouth and breathe through nose when requested for 2–3 minutes.

5. Oral Sensitivity

A. Gag reflex:
Gagged when touched tongue tip.

B. Reaction to oral sensory input:
Resistant to touch around and inside the mouth, defensive to touch.

C. Food texture/temperature:
Prefers thin purée foods, room temperature, crunchy solids.

D. Food texture/temperature:
Avoids mashed lumpy/ground food, hot, or cold temperatures.

Figure 5.3. Oral structures/movement worksheet completed for RT (*cont.*)
Source: Revised from Flanagan, 2008. Used with permission.

6. Descriptions of Movements While:

A. Drinking:
Prefers vanilla nutrition shake, also drinks water.

   1. Breast/Bottle:
   N/A

   2. Cup:
   Holds cup back in mouth, biting on cup edge.

      a. Lips:
      Whole mouth closes on cup, no separate lip movement.

      b. Tongue:
      Held back in the mouth while drinking.

      c. Jaw:
      Wide mouth opening for the cup.

      d. Swallow:
      Two to three sips, gulping sounds, some liquid loss from mouth corners.

   3. Straw:
   N/A

B. Spoon Food:
Thin purée at room temperature.

   1. Lips:
   No separate lip movement onto the spoon, whole mouth closes on spoon.

   2. Tongue:
   Held back in the mouth.

   3. Jaw:
   Wide mouth opening for the spoon.

   4. Swallow:
   Forward/backward movement of the tongue with a bunched tongue posture.

Figure 5.3. Oral structures/movement worksheet completed for RT (*cont.*)
Source: Revised from Flanagan, 2008. Used with permission.

---

7. Classification of Movement Patterns:

A. Typical Development:

B. Reflexive/Primitive:

C. Delayed:
  Biting on the cup edge, wide mouth opening with cup and spoon, lack of separate lip movements on cup and spoon, liquid loss with cup, for thin purée foods.

D. Atypical:
  Tongue held back in the mouth, lack of lateral tongue movement while chewing, gagging when touch tongue tip, gulping with swallow of liquid with two or three sip/swallows, swallowing with forward/backward movement with a bunched tongue posture. Unaware of food loss, refusal of hot/cold food temperatures, chewing only crunchy solids, primarily a mouth breather, resistant to touch around and inside the mouth, thick/bunched tongue posture, tight/thin lips with reduced range of motion of upper/lower lips, high/narrow palate, wide jaw movements and compensatory movement patterns while imitating simple movements.

Figure 5.3. Oral structures/movement worksheet completed for RT (*cont.*)
Source: Revised from Flanagan, 2008. Used with permission.

The information presented in this chapter is essential for building the child's treatment program. The information compiled will identify the best environment to begin treatment (home, school, or clinic); the type, taste, temperature and texture of food that is preferred; the level of development of food intake; the oral movement patterns to inhibit and those to facilitate; and the strategies that will enable successful mealtimes. The strategies that might work best with the child are developed from the parent/caretaker interviews and direct observations. For example, the initial feeding session may be only 5 minutes because the parents reported that the child has difficulty sitting for more than this amount of time for any snack or meal. Any medical, physical, or behavioral issues are also now known and ready to be taken into consideration for the child's overall program. The SLP or OT is now ready to develop the child's treatment plan.

Chapter 6

Treatment Program

Information gathered during the assessment process is used to design the treatment program. That is, the data gained will help identify the aspects of the child's sensory and motor systems that need to be addressed, how often treatment is needed, where treatment should occur, and what strategies would be most beneficial for the individual child. In the case of RT, we learned that he needed to be in a quieter environment, preferably at a table by himself, because his sensory system was easily overwhelmed by too much input. Furthermore, in order for his meal and treatment to be successful at school, food and utensils had to be sent from home.

Developing better feeding skills is a gradual process, but with a consistent, structured program the child can make the changes needed for successful mealtimes. In this connection, it is important to remember that the eating problems the child is experiencing have been going on for a period of time and that it takes time for the child to change her eating habits, oral sensory system, and movement patterns. For example, it takes a typically developing baby 10–15 repeated exposures to a new food before she accepts it (Galle). Therefore, it is important to be patient and allow the process to work with children who have been diagnosed with a feeding disorder. With a structured treatment program, a child with ASD can improve his feeding skills; however, it is difficult to estimate how long this will take until it is seen how he is progressing with the program.

The treatment plan must include goals that work toward the development of the components of movement found in typical feeding development, specifically oral awareness, oral discrimination, oral stability, separation and grading of movements, and sequencing and combining of movements. The plan must also work toward increasing the child's exposure to new foods and helping the child develop a balanced diet.

It is important for the family to communicate to the service provider their priority for a long-term goal. Examples of long-term treatment goals include increasing exposure to different textures and variety of foods, accepting new foods, chewing hard solids, using a variety of utensils during mealtimes, and independently eating a meal.

Previous chapters have described typical oral movement development while eating, the sensory processing systems, approaches to preparing the child's sensory-motor system for the meal, and ways to manipulate the child's environment for the feeding process. All of this knowledge is needed to design an effective sensory-motor approach to treating a feeding disorder.

The following sequence for treatment is recommended:

1. Prepare the sensory-motor environment
2. Prepare the sensory and motor systems for eating
3. Identify the level to begin treatment
4. Treat the sensory-motor skills while eating a meal or snack

The Sensory-Motor Environment

Physical Environment

During the assessment, the mealtime environments are described in the food journal by the parents and caretakers and also observed by the therapist doing the evaluation. The best environment for the meal to take place is now selected based on the assessment results. This must be a positive setting that meets the child's individual needs. For RT, a stable seating arrangement was recommended for both settings, with him at a table and chair, sitting with both feet flat on the floor and his arms easily rested on the table.

A visual schedule or a timer can be selected to help the child to predict the order and length of the meal. RT's schedule showed the meal starting with the accepted thin puree identified in the food journal. This was slightly thickened with a non-flavored thickener. This was followed by his preferred food, a barbecue chip, also identified in the food journal. A break was placed on the schedule. A timer was set for 5 minutes for the initial session.

Sensory Environment

During the assessment, the SLP, OT, parents, teachers, and other caretakers obtain information and directly observe how the child reacts to sensory information in different environments and with different individuals. The amounts of auditory, visual, olfactory, gustatory, proprioceptive, and tactile input must be adjusted to meet the child's needs during each snack or meal.

With RT, it was observed and reported that at school, he did best with the thin purée when seated at a separate table from his classmates. He was able to eat his preferred food with the group. At home, he sat at the family table for the thin purée and preferred food but left prior to the end of the meal. A separate table was recommended for school and home with his modified or new food. RT will not be expected to follow the treatment goals at the family meal or at the group table until he is successful at the separate table.

A Sensory-Motor Approach

After setting up the child's physical and sensory environment, it is time to prepare the child's sensory and motor systems for eating.

Sensory Play

Sensory play, as presented in Chapter Three, provides stimulation to touch, smell, taste, as well as the vestibular and proprioceptive systems. This can assist with the acceptance of new foods by helping the child to calm, organize, and alert her sensory system (Yack et al.). These activities should be part of the child's treatment program prior to the meal or snack to help organize and calm her for eating.

During the assessment process, it was discovered that RT did not like getting food on his hands and face and needed to smell food before eating. Sensory play activities were recommended by the SLP for RT prior to meals and snacks at home and school. One recommendation was to try homemade play dough with a variety of colors and smells added. RT was encouraged to interact with the play dough by squeezing, banging, rolling, and pushing it through a play dough device that changed the shape. Because it was homemade and did not contain any dangerous ingredients, it was okay if he put it in his mouth. A tactile bin was also presented to RT that contained items he could put in his mouth, such as marshmallows, along with a smelling box consisting of small bottles containing different scents (Yack et al.). He did not put the food into his mouth but he did touch the food to his lips and smell the bottles of scents. All of these activities helped to prepare him for the meal.

Oral Sensory Diet

The Oral Sensory Diet is an important part of a sensory-motor approach because it prepares the child for oral movement. It is based on predictable touch input that is presented in an acceptable manner to the child. The Oral Sensory Diet is preferably offered prior to a meal or snack but can initially be presented to the child in a play setting (Twachtman-Reilly et al.). This oral input will help the child interpret and discriminate the sensory-motor information received while moving the oral structures. This information can then be more easily remembered and used again during the mealtime (Flanagan). A list of materials for the Oral Sensory Diet may be found in Chapter Three.

An Oral Sensory Diet was recommended as part of RT's treatment program to prepare his oral structures due to his mouthing of objects, stuffing food into his mouth, poor awareness of a messy face, and difficulty accepting textured food. It was put on his schedule prior to meals and snacks both at school and at home. A schedule for the Oral Sensory Diet was used so he could see the sequence of activities being presented.

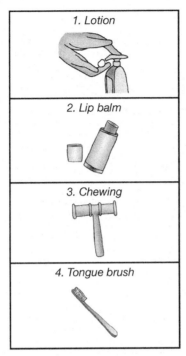

Figure 6.1. Visual schedule.
Symbols courtesy of Lessonpix.

Lotion was the first part of the diet, recommended for all body parts but especially the feet, hands, and face. The lotion was offered to RT in the same way each time so he could predict the manner and sequence of events. He was also encouraged to smell the lotion. This helped to prepare him for accepting input around and inside of his mouth. It was essential that he was seated in a stable position for the Oral Sensory Diet so as to maximize his acceptance of it.

After the lotion, tactile stimulation to the lips through use of lip balm and a soft washcloth were presented. This helped increase his oral awareness and decrease tactile sensitivity. A mini massager was offered but was rejected. A chew tube (www.chewytubes.com) was introduced to increase oral stability. RT was encouraged to chew with continuous, rhythmical movements for 10–30 times on each side. Counting helped him keep the beat and also to know how many times he had left to chew on each side. The adult working with RT placed a finger under his chin to help him grade the size of his mouth opening while chewing. This was needed because of the wide mouth opening observed during the assessment. The fourth activity on the schedule was use of the ARK Probe (www.arktherapeutic. com) to assist with oral awareness and facilitation of separate tongue movement. Poor oral awareness and a lack of separate tongue movements were both observed during the assessment.. The teachers and parents were instructed by the SLP to push down on the front half of the tongue for 10–30 times while his tongue was inside of his mouth. The adult working with RT again placed a finger under the chin to assist with maintaining a small mouth opening. The ARK Probe was also used to brush the sides of RT's tongue and then moved toward the side teeth to encourage lateral tongue movement. His tongue did follow the ARK Probe to either side. The same strategy was used with the blade and tip of the tongue. The ARK Probe touched the tongue and then moved to the palate, encouraging RT to follow it with his tongue to the top of his mouth to encourage separation of tongue movement from the lower jaw. RT did not follow the ARK Probe to the palate with his tongue blade or tongue tip.

After setting up the physical and sensory environment, preparing the child's sensory systems and organizing the oral tactile system, treatment is ready to begin at the appropriate level of development for the child so he can experience success at the snack or meal.

Treatment Plan

Based on the information gathered during the assessment, the SLP or OT is able to identify the types of movement patterns the child is using for semi-solids, solids, and liquids, as well as the skills needed to be successful during the treatment sessions.

During the assessment, it was noted that RT, exhibited oral hypersensitivity, mouth breathing, delayed movement patterns, and atypical movement patterns. He only tolerated one brand of store-bought baby foods, which was thin purée. RT needed to smell his food prior to feeding himself from a spoon. He drank a protein drink from a cup but with the cup held back in the mouth, inactive upper-lip movement, and audible swallows. RT preferred one type and brand of crunchy solid. He frequently stuffed large amounts of chips in his mouth. He exhibited a limited range of movement of the upper and lower lips and cheeks. The tongue was held back in the mouth with a bunched posture. There was reduced awareness of the oral structures, inadequate oral stability, a lack of separation of movements, and poor grading of the oral structures.

The following section describes a treatment plan for RT who is currently functioning at a 4 to 6-month level with a spoon food.

Spoon Feeding: 4–6 Months

Because RT only accepted thin purée foods from a spoon during the assessment, his level of development for spoon feeding would be at 4–6 months. This is identified as a delayed movement pattern because he is actually 5 years of age. At this stage of development, he would be expected to show the following skills:

- Open the mouth in anticipation of the spoon with tongue resting in mouth. RT uses a wide mouth opening with the tongue held back in the mouth.
- Close mouth on the spoon.
- Combination of forward/backward and vertical tongue movements.

Children functioning at the 4 to 6-month level typically accept a variety of puréed foods and explore the environment by putting objects and their hands in their mouths. RT did not go through the stage of oral exploration at 4–6 months and now resists tactile input around and inside of the mouth, stuffs large amounts of food in his mouth, and excessively provides himself with oral stimulation, including mouthing inedible objects. These reactions are indicative of an atypical sensory-motor feedback system that causes RT to only accept smooth foods.

Spoon Feeding: 7–9 Months

To work toward a 7 to 9-month level of development, treatment would facilitate acceptance of a thick purée with RT. Thick purée, typically eaten by 6 months of age, is a thickened, smooth food without lumps. Examples include blended meats, fruits, vegetables, and thickened cereals. The oral movements typically observed in a child who is able to eat a thick purée are as follows:

- The ability to quiet the mouth and begin to use upper-lip movement to clean the spoon.

- Continued combination of forward/backward and up/down tongue movement.

- The ability to tolerate increased sensation on the tongue as thicker food drops onto the tongue.

- Increased movements with the tongue and lips while taking food from the spoon.

The child's ability to quietly hold the mouth open in anticipation of the spoon and begin to use upper-lip movement to clean the spoon shows the development of oral stability and separation of movement. The ability to tolerate the thickened texture indicates increased oral awareness and discrimination. These are the skills that would be emphasized in treatment with RT, who continues to only tolerate a thin purée, in order to move him to the next level of development. An atypical sensory motor system was also noted with RT because of his acceptance of only one type of puréed food and resistance to oral tactile input. These atypical responses must be addressed during treatment through consistent use of the Oral Sensory Diet, sensory play activities, and gradual varying of the thickness of the puréed food. His wide mouth opening for the spoon, with the tongue held back in the mouth, must also be focused on during his therapy session by using jaw control or verbal cues.

Liquid Intake: 7–9 Months

At the 7 to 9-month stage of development, the child should show the following skills with the bottle and cup:

- Active center lip movement on the nipple.

- Drink 7 to 8 oz. at a time from a bottle.

- Rhythmical suck/swallow pattern with a strong suck.

- No loss from the mouth corners with the bottle.

- Drinking one to three sips from a cup.

- Liquid loss while drinking from the cup.

RT's drinking skills are at a 7 to 9-month level. Because he is chronologically older than this, he is exhibiting delayed movement patterns. Treatment with RT's drinking skills would work toward facilitating movements at the next level of development, 10–12 months.

Liquid Intake: 10–12 Months

The goals for this level would be for RT to:

- Drink three sips from the cup with no liquid loss or gulping sounds.

- Control liquid loss so it is only seen with removal of the cup from the mouth.

- Grade the size of the mouth opening for the cup.

- Continue to hold the cup back in the mouth, if needed.

Development of these skills would indicate that the child's oral system is acquiring increased oral stability, oral awareness, and oral discrimination. A cause for concern would be if the child would only drink from one cup. This would be an example of an atypical pattern. This is the case with RT, so treatment would concentrate on presenting him with a variety of cups and utensils. This might begin with play with a variety of cups, spoons, forks, plates, and bowls at a separate time. A new utensil may also be introduced by placing it on the mealtime table without requiring him to use it. This will help RT become visually accustomed to it.

Solid Foods: 7–9 Months

In typical development, the 7 to 9-month-old child is:

- Eating finger foods.

- Accepting a variety of new foods with varied tastes, textures, and appearances.

RT is having difficulty chewing solid foods, because he is only accepting a particular crunchy solid. Many parents who have a child with ASD report their child prefers one type and brand of crunchy solid and resists eating other finger foods. Treatment with RT would work toward this 7 to 9-month level of development with solid foods. He would be encouraged to:

- Bite a soft solid.

- Eat a broader variety of crunchy solids by changing the flavor or the brand.

During the assessment, RT had difficulty with drinking skills as well as the intake of spoon foods and finger foods. He was reported and observed to only accept a particular brand of jarred, puréed baby food, take two to three sips from a cup with liquid loss, and accept only one type and brand of crunchy solid. He was assessed to be at a 4 to 6-month level with semi-solids and solid foods and a 7 to 9-month level with cup drinking skills. He displayed both delayed and atypical oral movement patterns. The treatment goals for RT are discussed in the following section.

Treatment Goals

The SLP or OT can now develop RT's treatment goals and strategies. It is important to prioritize goals. For example, he should be working toward only two to three goals at a time to avoid the child, family, and other caretakers becoming overwhelmed (Ernsperger & Stegen-Hanson). The goals should be specific (Galle) to make it possible to take data on each goal as a way to monitor when changes need to be made to his feeding plan (Bruns & Thompson). In other words, the data will tell when the plan is going well and when changes need to be made.

A long-term goal for RT would be to increase the variety of foods eaten at snacks and meals.

Short-term goals for RT would be:

- To eat an accepted smooth food from the spoon that has been thickened with a non-flavored thickener during a snack.

- To eat a new smooth food from the spoon during a snack.

- To eat a new crunchy solid during a snack.

- To grade the size of the mouth opening for the spoon and cup.

- To produce downward upper-lip movement on the spoon and cup edge.

Treatment Strategies

When working on the first short-term goal, it is important to initially present a small portion size to RT so that he does not get overwhelmed and reject the food before trying it. At first, a teaspoon of the new food is tried. In this case, the new food is a preferred smooth food that has been thickened. The food can be thickened slightly to start and then slowly increased in texture over the course of the treatment sessions. The new food should be introduced on a daily basis so that he can become desensitized to the look, smell, and touch of it. A first step to facilitating an "adaptive orienting response" to a novel food might be to simply encourage the child to look at it or smell it. The olfactory or smell system is closely related to the gustatory or taste system. Encouraging him to smell the new food may facilitate his willingness to accept and taste it. A small amount of the new food could be placed on the table while RT is eating an accepted food. He would be encouraged to allow the new food to stay on table. The next step might be to put the new food on the plate with the accepted food. The only expectation would be that the new food stays on the plate (Wheeler). This could follow the five stages of sensory development for tolerating new foods (acceptance, touch, smell, taste, and eating) described by Ernsperger and Stegen-Hanson.

During the initial session, RT did pick up the spoon and touch the thickened purée to his tongue. He was then given a barbecue potato chip.

Another strategy would be to pair new foods with accepted foods. Begin by offering more of the accepted food than the new food. For example, place the accepted food on the front of the spoon with the new food on the back. Gradually fade out the accepted food.

For the second short-term goal, the sensory qualities of the new food should be as close as possible to those of an accepted food—in color, taste, and texture. One way to change the accepted food is to vary the brand or flavor. For example, RT is accepting only one brand of jarred food. This could be varied by using another brand of the jarred food or the same brand but a new flavor. This way the color and texture stay the same, the only difference would be the flavor or the brand. The texture of an accepted food can be changed by slowly adding graham cracker crumbs to it. Finally, changing the temperature of an accepted food could also make it a new food. Children with ASD tend to prefer foods that are room temperature. The temperature of the food could be gradually lowered or raised. Changing only one aspect of the accepted food makes it easier to positively respond to it as a new food.

The size of the plate or bowl also needs to be considered. It might be better to start with a smaller bowl and a lunch or salad plate instead of a dinner plate (Ernsperger & Stegen-Hanson). The cup and eating utensils also need to be the right size for him. Also, the number of foods presented at the meal should be limited to two to three. For example, this could be the new food and the preferred food.

Many children with ASD have a deficient arousal modulating system, which may be exhibited as either an under- or an overreaction to sensory stimuli. A child who is underreactive to sensory stimuli may accept a new food with a strong flavor, such as spicy foods, so the taste can be registered by the child's system. The child who overreacts to sensory stimuli might need a new food to have less flavor (Bruns & Thompson). RT seemed to like strong flavors with his barbecue potato chips. His feeding program could attempt to increase the flavor of the jarred baby food by adding puréed table food to it.

Allowing RT to assist with the food preparation might help to create a positive atmosphere (Bodison et al.). Children also learn by observing others. RT may be more likely to eat the novel food if he sees another eating the food while stating how much she likes it (Galle).

For the third short-term goal, some of the techniques used with the spoon food can be applied to the presentation of a new finger food. The sensory qualities of the new finger food should be as close as possible to those of the accepted food in color, taste, and texture. This may be accomplished by changing the brand or one aspect of the preferred food. For example, RT could be presented with a new flavor of potato chips. Another way to create a new food might be to change the appearance of an accepted food. For example, an accepted sandwich or chicken nuggets could be cut into different shapes. With all new foods presented, the portion size should be small.

These short-term goals are attainable because they are starting at RT's current level of functioning and working toward the next developmental level. Consistency and repetition are also important factors for the child's success with these goals. The use of rewards, prompts, and visual schedules may also be necessary for a successful mealtime.

Reinforcement

Feelings of hunger and the taste of the food may not be enough to prompt the child with ASD to eat something novel. Therefore, the first task is to find out what the child likes and is willing to work for. This could be a highly preferred food. Use of preferred foods as a reward may lead to the acceptance of new foods. The reward should be given immediately after eating a small portion of the targeted food. At first, the child is required to only eat a small amount of the food. As the child accepts the food, more of it is required to receive the reward (Galle). A first-then board may be used, showing a picture of the new food under the word "FIRST" and the preferred food under the word "THEN." It must be clear to the child that he must eat the new food in order to get the reward. This is reinforced through repeated use of the first-then board. If the child is resistant to eating the new food, then the feeding specialist may need to change the level of expectation to where the child is now tolerating the new food. For example, the child may only smell the new food. The child might taste the new food but not put it in her mouth. The goal would be to work toward eating the new food. This preferred food should not be used outside of the meal with the child. Also, preferences can change over time with the child and must be reassessed on a regular basis.

Prompts

Prompts may also be used to help the child accept the targeted food. Verbal prompts should be simple statements delivered in a calm voice at regular intervals.

For example, "Put the _____ in your mouth." The verbal prompt "Use a small mouth" was initially used with RT because he was sensitive to touch with jaw control. Physical gestures, such as pointing, may also be used as prompts. In addition, a timer can serve as a prompt so the child knows the beginning and the end of the meal. The maximum length of the snack should be 15 minutes. A meal should not be longer than 30 minutes (Galle).

Schedules

A daily schedule can help the child know when the snack or meal is going to occur during the child's day. A mealtime schedule, in turn, would indicate the order of foods presented to the child during the meal. This will not only help the child know what food to expect but also the length of the meal or snack. This would be indicated by how many times the new food and preferred food occurs on the schedule.

Figure 6.2 is an example of a daily schedule. The picture symbol on the left is moved to the middle column to show the activity is happening now. The picture symbol is moved to the column on the right to show when it is over. The next picture in the left column is then moved up to indicate that it is the next activity to occur with the child. More pictures can be stored on the back of the schedule on a Velcro strip or in an attached pouch.

WILL DO	DOING	DONE
math class		
reading class		
oral motor		
lunch		

Figure 6.2. Daily schedule.

Figure 6.3 is a mealtime schedule, which lets the child know the sequence of foods during a snack. If necessary, a format similar to the daily schedule can be used with the mealtime schedule. It might be enough for the sequence events to be shown to the child as they occur. A daily schedule and a mealtime schedule were both used with RT.

Figure 6.3. Mealtime schedule.
Symbols courtesy of Lessonpix.

In summary, the goal of the child's treatment plan is to increase a more typical motor response by manipulating the sensory environment (Alexander, Boehme & Cupps, 1982). The manipulation of the sensory environment inhibits delayed, primitive, compensatory, or atypical movement patterns, facilitates the underlying components of oral movements, and makes possible more typical movement patterns. Alexander, Boehme & Cupps (2011) stated that by facilitating these movement patterns, we are increasing the child's options for selecting successful actions. Daily treatment and manipulation of the sensory environment enable the child to move to the next developmental level with her feeding skills. Patience is needed while working with the child. It is important to initially present small amounts of food and keep treatment sessions short. Treatment will also be more successful when it includes everyone who is involved with her meals. The ultimate long-term goal is to enable the mealtime experience to be successful and enjoyable for all as well as for the increased welfare and health of the child (Bodison et al.).

Chapter 7

Sensory Activities for the Home and School

Sensory activities that are part of the routine of home and school help ensure generalization and greater success with the goals that are being addressed during the feeding program. Not all of the activities listed will be helpful with every child. An intervention may work well one day but not the next. It is best to try different activities and observe the child's behavior, selecting the activity that works best at the time (Kerstein).

Alerting Activities

Alerting activities are helpful for a child who is under-responsive or hypo-responsive to stimuli. Examples of under-responsive behaviors include being excessively quiet and shut down or seeking strong sensations. The activities listed here may help the child become more responsive to sensory stimuli and therefore show less sensory-seeking behaviors. Becoming more aware and ready to act will enable the child to respond to situations in a more appropriate manner such as the snack or mealtime setting. Try to engage the child in some of these activities prior to meal or snack time or at other times during the day (Kerstein).

- Listening to music with a beat for attention and focus/moving to music
- Going for a walk around the block
- Wiping the child's face with a wet washcloth
- Using face paints/makeup, possibly in front of a mirror
- Bouncing on a ball
- Spinning on a Sit'n'Spin
- Catching or throwing a ball
- Blowing bubbles, whistles, cotton balls
- Chewing on gum or mouth tools
- Tasting sour, spicy, or bitter things
- Eating frozen or cold foods such as juice bars
- Doing cold water play
- Using vibration with toy massagers
- Jumping on a mini trampoline
- Smelling peppermint and citrus
- Doing finger play and singing interactive songs ("Ring Around the Rosie," "Five Little Monkeys," "Humpty Dumpty")

Tony was lying on the floor prior to lunch. It was difficult for the teachers to engage him and persuade him to sit up. His teacher began to blow bubbles on his hands, arms, and legs to make him more alert. Tony finally stood up and began reaching and popping the bubbles. He was also given a straw and cotton ball to blow across the table as well as a variety of whistles. After blowing the cotton balls and whistles, he walked independently to the table for the Oral Sensory Diet and lunch.

There were similar problems sustaining an alert state with Tony at home. The family began to take a walk prior to meals, which was placed on his daily schedule at home. Tony actually began to look forward to his walk, which became a good family interaction time. After the walk, he readily sat at his table for his Oral Sensory Diet and meal. On rainy days he jumped on a mini trampoline instead.

Calming Activities

Calming activities are helpful for a child who is hyper-responsive to sensory input, causing her to be in a heightened state. This child may quickly move from one activity to another without engaging with anything presented to her. Ideally, these activities are presented to the child before stimuli become too overwhelming to her and assist the child with regulating her responses to sensory input. These interventions can be regularly placed on the child's schedule prior to a snack or meal.

- Reading a book about food / eating
- Wrapping up in a blanket
- Washing the table and / or chair for the meal
- Carrying or pushing heavier items (pushing the chair over to the table)
- Using firm, rhythmical pressure with the child while seated in a beanbag chair or large pillows
- Rolling a weighted ball back and forth
- Using a weighted lap pad
- Slow rocking in a rocking chair or swing
- Taking a warm bath (Kranowitz)
- Soothing smells such as lavender or vanilla (Yack et al.)
- Hugging a pillow or stuffed animal (Yack et al.)
- Sitting in a quiet room with low lights

Mary had trouble sitting or standing still when in a heightened, alert state. She frequently laughed and quickly moved about the room, making it difficult for her to focus. She enjoyed water play, so a job where she washed the lunch table and chair was put on her schedule prior to the Oral Sensory Diet and

*lunch. This sensory activity helped her become focused and ready for the meal-
time experience.*

*At home, Mary was given a warm bath prior to dinner, even if she was
not in a heightened state. The bath helped her regulate her reactions to sensory
stimulation during the meal so there was a greater possibility for success.*

Organizing Activities

The following interventions help reduce anxiety and increase attention to
relevant information. An organized and attentive state will increase success
during the meal. They can easily be worked into the child's daily tasks and
routines.

- Sucking hard candies (Yack et al.)
- Chewing on crunchy solids and / or mouth tools
- Blowing activities
- Using toy massagers (Yack et al.)
- Carrying heavier objects
- Providing compressions into the joints (Yack et al.)
- Sucking from a water bottle or through a straw

*Eddie and his classmates had a water bottle at their desks and were allowed
to take drinks throughout the day. This kept them hydrated and organized for
their daily tasks. Eddie needed more input, so a small plastic tube was placed
over the eraser on his pencil. Chewing on this helped him maintain an organized, alert state throughout the day.*

Case Story

Based on information from the assessment and direct observations, activities that were calming to RT were added to the sensory play activities men-
tioned in Chapter Six. A visual symbol for each activity was placed on his
schedule both at home and school.

RT enjoyed sitting in a beanbag chair, so this type of seating was selected
for use during the Oral Sensory Diet. A weighted lap pad was placed on his

lap to help him feel calm and safe in his body. The room was quiet, with low lighting to decrease overstimulation by visual and auditory input. The Oral Sensory Diet as outlined in Chapter Three was done while he was in the beanbag chair. After the Oral Sensory Diet, RT pushed his chair over to a small table for the snack or meal.

Chapter 8

Summary and Conclusions

The diagnostic criteria for ASD listed in DSM-5 (American Psychiatric Association, p. 50) under the category of "restricted, repetitive patterns of behavior, interests or activities" contain the following statement: "hyper- or hypo-reactivity to sensory input or unusual interest in sensory aspects of the environment." This includes unpleasant responses to sounds and textures and extreme smelling and touching.

These new diagnostic criteria support a sensory-motor approach to a feeding treatment program. Many authors have agreed over the years that sensory processing issues are present in the child with ASD (Nadon et al.). This is the first time it has been included among the criteria for a diagnosis of ASD.

Treating feeding skills in a child with a diagnosis of ASD is a complex process because of the many variables that can affect the child's success with a meal. The child needs an intervention program that follows typical development, begins at the child's current skill level, progresses in small increments, and is structured and predictable. Such an approach must prepare the child's sensory processing systems and motor systems as well as control the sensory and physical environments. All of these variables are part of the treatment program described throughout this book.

Parents, other caretakers, and teachers are important participants in the child's treatment program. Sensory activities that enhance the child's sensory processing skills need to be part of the routines both at home and at school. This will enable generalization of skills and greater success with the goals addressed during the feeding program. To that end, Chapter Seven lists activities that will assist with the child's ability to alert, calm, and organize, and can become part of the child's home and school routines. These will then stimulate success with the child's skills and behaviors during snacks and meals at home and school.

Many families who have a child with ASD need help with managing their child's diet as well as behaviors and skills related to eating. For many families, it is a challenge to go to restaurants, take vacations, or visit friends and family due to their child's feeding and eating issues. When deciding to start treatment, it is important for families to recognize that these behaviors have typically been occurring over a significant period of time and that therefore it will take time and patience to bring about change. The process is effective, but it takes consistent daily effort and participation by all involved: therapists, teachers, parents, caretakers, and the child.

References

Alexander, R., Boehme, R., & Cupps, B. (1982). *Early feeding, sound production, and pre-linguistic/cognitive development and their relationship to gross-motor and fine-motor development* [handout]. Wauwatosa, WI.

Alexander, R., Boehme, R., & Cupps, B. (2011). *Key characteristics of posture and movement.* Retrieved from www.ohioslha.org/pdf/Convention/2011%20Handouts/SC3DysphagiaAlexander.pdf Feb 15, 2011 ... OSLHA Convention - March 18, 2011...

American Psychiatric Association (2013). *Diagnostic and statistical manual of mental disorders* (5th ed.). Arlington, VA: Author.

Anderson, T. (2001, Sept 25). *Different types of exercise.* Retrieved from www.trulyhuge.com/news/tips55a.htm

Ayres, J. A. (2000). *Sensory integration and the child.* Los Angeles, CA: Western Psychological Services.

Bathel, J. A. (2006). Muscle-based approach to speech therapy. *Oral-Motor, 16*(48), 10. Retrieved from http://speech-language-pathology-audiology.advanceweb.com/article/oral-motor.aspx

Beckman, D. (1995a). Major brain centers for oral motor control. *Oral Motor Assessment & Intervention,* 11–12.

Beckman, D. (1995b). Oral-motor patterns. *Oral Motor Assessment & Intervention,* 20–31.

Blausen.com staff (2014). Blausen gallery 2014. *Wikiversity Journal of Medicine.* DOI:10.15347/wjm/2014. 010. ISSN 20018762.

Bodison, S., Hsu, V., Hurtubise, C., & Surfus, J. (2010). *Sensory integration: Answers for mealtime success.* Torrance, CA: Pediatric Therapy Network.

Brain Gym (2015). Ventura, CA: Brain Gym International/Educational Kinesiology Foundation. Retrieved from www.braingym.org.

Brack, J.C. (2009). *Learn to move, moving up! Sensorimotor elementary-school activity themes.* Shawnee Mission, KS: AAPC.

Bruns, D. A., & Thompson, S. (2011). Time to eat: improving mealtimes of young children with autism. *Young Exceptional Children, 14*(3), 3–15.

Bryan, L., & Gast, D.L. (2000). Teaching on task and on-schedule behaviors to high-functioning children with autism via picture activity schedules. *Journal of Autism and Developmental Disorders, 30*(6).

Cafiero, J. M. (2005). *Meaningful exchanges for people with autism.* Bethesda, MD: Woodbine House.

Clark, H. M. (2006). *Therapeutic exercise in dysphagia management: Philosophies, practices, and challenges.* Rockville, MD: Professional Development and Special Interest Division 13, Swallowing and Swallowing Disorders (Dysphagia), American Speech-Language-Hearing Association (ASHA).

Corbett, B. A., Mendoza, S., Abdull, M. Weyelin, J. & Levine, S. (2006). Cortisol circadian rhythms and response to stress in children with autism. *Psychoendocrinology, 31*(1), 59–68.

Courchesne, E., Lincoln, A. J., Kilman, B. A., & Galambos, R. (1985). Event-related brain potential correlates of the processing of novel visual and auditory information in autism. *Journal of Autism and Developmental Disorders, 15*(1), a55–a76.

Dawson, G. (1989). *Autism: Nature, diagnosis and treatment.* New York: Guilford Press.

Edelson, M. (1996). *Interview with Lorna Jean King: A pioneer of sensory integration therapy.* Retrieved from www.autism-help.org/points-lorna-jean-sensory.htm

Edmond, A., Emmett, P., Steer, C., & Golding, J. (2010). Feeding symptoms, dietary patterns and growth in young children with autism spectrum disorders. *Pediatrics, 126*(2), e337–e342.

Ernsperger, L., & Stegen-Hanson, T. (2004). *Just take a bite.* Arlington, TX: Future Horizons.

Escalona, A., Field, T., Singer-Strunck, R., Cullen, C., & Hartshorn, K. (2001). Brief report: improvement in children with autism following massage therapy. *Journal of Autism and Developmental Disorders, 31*(5), pp.513-516.

Evans-Morris, S., & Dunn-Klein, M. (2000). *Pre-feeding skills.* Tucson, AZ: Therapy Skill Builders.

Flanagan, M. A. (2008). *Improving speech and eating skills in children with autism spectrum disorders.* Shawnee Mission, KS: AAPC.

Gagnon, D. E. (1999). *Tone versus strength.* Retrieved from http://www.myteacherpages.com/webpages/schynoweth/files/tone%20versus%20strength.doc

Galle, J. (2010). *What to do when a child won't eat: Feeding disorders & developmental disabilities.* Retrieved from http//www.centerforautism.com/Data/Sites/1/media/Feeding-Presentation-South-Africa-1.pdf

Henry, S., & Myles, B. S. (2014). *The comprehensive autism planning system (CAPS) for individuals with autism spectrum disorders and related disabilities: Integrating evidence-based practices throughout the student's day.* Shawnee Mission, KS: AAPC.

Hoekman, L. A. (2005). *Sensory integration.* Retrieved from www.thegraycenter.org/sensory_integration.htm.

Hoopes, A., & Applebaum, S. A. (2009). *Eye power: A cutting edge report on vision therapy.* Charleston, SC: BookSurge.

Kaplan, M. (2006). *Seeing through new eyes: Changing the lives of children with autism, Asperger syndrome and other developmental disabilities through vision therapy.* Philadelphia, PA: Jessica Kingsley.

Kerstein, L. H. (2008). *My sensory book: Working together to explore sensory issues and the big feelings they can cause: a workbook for parents, professionals, and children.* Shawnee Mission, KS: AAPC.

King, L. J. (1991). Sensory integration: An effective approach to therapy and education. *Autism Research Review International, 5,* 2.

King, L. J. (2007–2008). *An interview with Lorna Jean King, OTR, FAOTA.* Retrieved from http:www.autism-help.org/points-lorna-jean-sensory.htm.

King, L. J. (2009). *Understanding proprioception.* Retrieved from http://devdelay.org/newsletter/articles/html/97/lorna-jean-king.html.

Kranowitz, C. (2006). *The out-of-sync child.* New York: The Penguin Group.

Kumin, L. (2002). Developmental apraxia of speech in children and adults with Down syndrome. *Disability Solutions, 5,* 1–15.

Lawrence, M. (1971). Mechanics of the ear. In L. E. Travis (Ed.), *Handbook of speech pathology and audiology* (pp. 245–261). New York: Meredith Corp, Appleton-Century-Crofts Educational Division.

Lazarus, C. L. (2006). *Lingual strengthening and swallowing*. Rockville, MD: Professional Development & Special Interest Division 13, Swallowing and Swallowing Disorders (Dysphagia), American Speech-Language-Hearing Association (ASHA).

Legge, B. (2002). *Can't eat, won't eat*. Philadelphia, PA: Jessica Kingsley.

Legisa, J., Messinger, D.S., Kermol, E., & Marlier, L. (2013). Emotional responses to odors in children with high-functioning autism: Autonomic arousal, facial behavior and self-report. *Journal of Autism and Developmental Disorders, 43*(4), 869-879.

McCarthy, J. (2008). Feeding infants and toddlers. *Strategies for safe, stress-free mealtimes*. Retrieved from http://www.asha.org/events/convention/handouts/2008/1884_mccarthy_jessica_1/

Myles, B.S., Mahler, K., & Robbins, L. A. (2014). *Sensory issues and high-functioning autism spectrum and related disorders: practical solutions for making sense of the world* (2nd ed.). Shawnee Mission, KS: AAPC.

Nadon, G, Feldman Ehrmann, D., Dunn, W., & Gisel, E. (2011). Association of sensory processing and eating problems in children with autism spectrum disorders. *Autism Research and Treatment, 2011*, 1–9.

OCALI. (2012). *Sensory and biological needs and strategies*. Retrieved from https://www.yumpu.com/en/document/view/24880751/pdf-ocali-sensory-ohio-center-for-autism-and-low-incidence.

Oetter, P., Richter, E., & Frick, S. (1995). *M.O.R.E.: Integrating the mouth with sensory and postural functions* (2nd ed.). Hugo, MN: PDP Press.

Pfeiffer, B., Koenig, K., Kinnealey, M., Sheppard, M., & Henderson, L. (2011). Effectiveness of sensory integration interventions in children with autism spectrum disorder: A pilot study. *American Journal of Occupational Therapy, 65*, 76–85.

Potock, M. (2010). *Happy mealtimes with happy kids: How to teach your child about the joy of food*. Longmont, CO: My Munch Bug Publishing.

Redstone, F. (2004). The importance of postural control for feeding in children with neurogenic disorders. *Pediatric Nursing, 30*(2), 97–100.

Rogers, L. G., Magill-Evans, J., Rempel, G. R. (2011). Mothers' challenges in feeding their children with autism spectrum disorder-managing more than just picky eating. *Journal of Development and Physical Disabilities, 24*, 19–33.

Salek, B. (1975). *Normal motor development as a base for normal respiration and pre-speech function.* Baltimore, MD: University of Maryland Medical School, Department of Physical Therapy.

Sayers, B. (2008). *Improving speech and eating skills.* Retrieved from http://www.bellaonline.org/articles/art57942.asp

Sears, R. W. (2010). *The autism book: What every parent needs to know about early detection, treatment, recovery, and prevention.* New York: Little, Brown & Co.

Sheppard, J. J. (2006). *The role of oral sensorimotor therapy in the treatment of pediatric dysphagia.* Rockville, MD: Professional Development and Special Interest Division 13, Swallowing and Swallowing Disorders (Dysphagia), American Speech-Language-Hearing (ASHA).

Talk Autism. (2007). *The sensory world.* Retrieved from sites.google.com/site/talkautism/thesensoryworld

Thornton, M. (2003). *Review — Can't eat, won't eat: Dietary difficulties and the autism spectrum by Brenda Legge.* Retrieved from http://metapsychology.mentalhelp.net/poc/view_doc.php?type=book&id=1527

Tomchek, S. D., & Dunn, W. (2007). Sensory processing in children with and without autism: a comparative study using the short sensory profile. *American Journal of Occupational Therapy, 61,* 190–200.

Travis, L. (1971). *Handbook of speech pathology and audiology.* New York: Appleton-Century-Crofts Educational Division.

Trivedi, B. P. (2012). Gustatory system: The finer points of taste. *Nature, 486* (7403), S2-S3.

Twachtman-Reilly, J., Amaral, S. C., & Zebrowski, P. (2008). Addressing feeding disorders in children on the autism spectrum in school-based settings: Physiological and behavioral issues. *Language, Speech and Hearing Services in Schools, 39,* 261–272.

Upledger, J. (1996). *A brain is born.* Berkeley, CA: North Atlantic Books.

WebMD (2012). *Dental health and your child's teeth.* Retrieved from http://www.webmd.com/oral-health/guide/dental-health-your-childs-teeth.

Wheeler, M. (2004). Mealtime and children on the autism spectrum: Beyond picky, fussy and fads. *The Reporter, 9*(2), 13–19.

Williams, K.E., & Seiverling, L. (2010). Eating problems in children with autism spectrum disorders. *Topics in Clinical Nutrition, 25*(1), 27-37.

Yack, E., Aquilla, P., & Sutton, S. (2015). *Building bridges through sensory integration: Therapy for children with autism and other pervasive developmental disorders*. Arlington, TX: Future Horizons.

Yost, W. A. (2002). Auditory perception. In *The Encyclopedia of the Human Brain* (Vol 1, A-Cog, pp. 303–320). New York: Academic Press.

Additional Resources

Books

The following is a list of resource books, many of which have been cited in this book. All contain information helpful to anyone working with a child with ASD and would be a beneficial addition to a reference library.

Ayres, J. (1979). *Sensory integration and the child*. Los Angeles, CA: Western Psychological Services.

Brack, J.C. (2009). *Learn to move, moving up!* Shawnee Mission, KS: AAPC.

Cafiero, J. M. (2005). *Meaningful exchanges for people with autism: An introduction to augmentative & alternative communication*. Bethesda, MD: Woodbine House.

Ernsperger, L., & Stegen-Hanson, T. (2004). *Just take a bite*. Arlington, TX: Future Horizons.

Evans-Morris, S., & Dunn-Klein, M. (2000). *Pre-feeding skills*. Tucson, AZ: Therapy Skill Builders.

Flanagan, M. (2008). *Improving speech and eating skills in children with autism spectrum disorders: An oral-motor program for home and school*. Shawnee Mission, KS: AAPC.

Gray, C. (2010). *The new Social Story book*. Arlington, TX: Future Horizons.

Gray, C. (1994). *Comic strip conversations*. Arlington, TX: Future Horizons.

Henry, S., & Myles, B. S. (2014). *The comprehensive autism planning system (CAPS) for individuals with autism spectrum disorders and related disabilities: Integrating evidence-based practices throughout the student's day* (2nd ed.). Shawnee Mission, KS: AAPC.

Kerstein, L. H. (2008). *My sensory book: Working together to explore sensory issues and the big feelings they can cause*. Shawnee Mission, KS: AAPC.

Myles, B.S., Mahler, K., & Robbins, L. A. (2014). *Sensory issues and high-functioning autism spectrum and related disorders: Practical solutions for making sense of the world*. Shawnee Mission, KS: AAPC.

Sears, R.W. (2010). *The autism book: What every parent needs to know about early detection, treatment, recovery, and prevention.* New York: Little, Brown & Co.

Yack, E., Aquilla, P., & Sutton, S. (2002). *Building bridges through sensory integration: Therapy for children with autism and other pervasive developmental disorders.* Arlington, TX: Future Horizons.

Organizations

American Speech/Language Hearing Association:
The professional association for speech-language pathologists, audiologists, and speech, language and hearing scientist. 10801 Rockville Pike, Rockville, MD 20852; (800) 638-8255; www.asha.org

Brain Gym International:
A nonprofit corporation that promotes movement-based programs that lead to optimal learning. 1575 Spinaker Drive, Suite 204 B, Ventura, CA 93001; (800) 356-2109; www.braingym.com

Companies That Sell Oral-Motor Products/Symbols

ARK Therapeutic Services, Inc.:
Utensils and oral-motor products. 862-A Highway 1 South, P.O. Box 340, Lugoff, SC 29078; (803) 438-9779; www.arktherapeutic.com

Beyond Play, LLC:
Sensory products, utensils, and oral-motor products. 1442A Walnut Street, Berkeley, CA 84709; (877) 428-1244; Fax: (877) 218-8441; custserv@beyondplay.com

Chewy Tubes:
Oral-motor products. P.O. Box 2289, So. Portland, ME; (207) 741-2443; Fax: (207) 799-2289; info@chewytubes.com

Lessonpix:
Clip-art website to assist with creating lesson materials. 35246 US Hwy 19 N #139, Palm Harbor, FL 34684; (727) 437-2465; www.lessonpix.com

Pocket Full of Therapy:
Sensory and oral-motor products. P.O. Box 174, Morganville, NJ 07751; (732) 441-1422; www.pfot.com

Southpaw Enterprises:
Sensory materials, seating options, and oral-motor products. P.O. Box 1047, Dayton, OH 45401-1047; (800) 228-1698; www.southpawenterprises.com

Super Duper Publications:
Utensils and oral-motor products. Dept. SD 2008, P.O. Box 24997, Greenville, SC 29616-2497; (800) 277-8737; www.superduperinc.com

The Speech Bin:
Oral-motor products. P.O. Box 922668, Norcross, GA 30010-2668; (800) 850-8602; www.speechbin.com

Therapy Shoppe, Inc.:
Sensory/oral-motor products and utensils. P.O. Box 8875, Grand Rapids, MI 49518; (800) 261-5590; www.therapyshoppe.com

Appendix

Developmental Feeding Questionnaire

Oral Structures/Oral Movement Worksheet

Developmental Feeding Questionnaire

Name:	Birthday:
Age:	Date:
Diagnosis:	

1. Did you breastfeed your child right after birth?

    A. How long did it take your child to breastfeed?

    B. Until what age did your child breastfeed?

    C. Was there a difficulty that caused you to bottle feed?

2. If bottle fed, what type of nipple was used with your child?

    A. How long did it take for your child to complete an 8-ounce bottle?

    B. What age did you stop breastfeeding or bottle feeding?

3. At what age did your child:
    A. Accept solid food from a spoon?

- What type of food was first accepted by your child?

- What type of spoon was used?

- Does your child feed him-/herself with a spoon?

    B. Accept textured food from a spoon?

- What type of textured food is accepted by spoon (mashed lumpy, ground food)?

    C. Eat table foods?

- What type of food did he/she first accept?

- What type of food does he/she accept now?

- Did he/she refuse any type of table food?

Source: Bruns & Thompson, 2011. Used with permission.

Developmental Feeding Questionnaire (*cont.*)

3. At what age did your child (*cont.*):
C. Eat table foods?

- What type of food did he/she first accept?

- What type of food does he/she accept now?

- Did he/she refuse any type of table food?

D. Finger feed table foods?

- What type of food did he/she first accept? (crunchy, soft, or hard)

- What type of food does he/she accept now?

- Did he/she refuse any or all types of finger food?

- Does your child chew finger foods?

- Does your child move foods side to side in the mouth?

- How long is a typical mealtime?

E. Drink from a cup (assisted and unassisted)?

- What liquids did he/she first accept? (water, juices, thickened drinks)

- What liquids does he/she accept now?

- What type of cup does he/she use?

F. Drink from a straw?

Developmental Feeding Questionnaire (*cont.*)

3. At what age did your child (*cont.*):
G. Become aware of food on his/her face?

- Does your child continue to be a messy eater?

- Does food fall out of his/her mouth?

- Does he/she store food in the cheeks?

H. Begin to feed him/herself?

- At what age did your child feed him/herself?

- How long does it take for your child to feed him/herself?

- What utensils can your child use?

I. Begin and stop exploring objects by mouth?

- Does your child put inedible objects in his/her mouth?

J. Begin and stop drooling?

- Does your child drool only at specific times?

4. Have there been concerns about your child's overall developmental growth?

5. Does your child accept new foods? Does he/she have a preference for a certain food group?

6. How many meals/snacks does your child eat in 1 day? Does your child sit at a table for meals?

7. What is your child's school history?

Medical History Questionnaire

Name:	Birthday:
Age:	Date:
Diagnosis:	

1. **Does your child have food allergies?**

   A. Is your child on a special diet?

   B. Has your child had a reaction to any foods?

2. **Has your child had a history of choking or gagging on food?**

   A. Has there been difficulty swallowing any foods or liquids?

   B. Has your child ever needed to receive tube feedings? (nasogastric or gastrostomy tube)

   C. Has food ever come out of your child's nose?

3. **Is your child a picky eater?**

4. **Does your child have any gastrointestinal problems such as reflux, diarrhea, or constipation?**

5. **Is your child taking any medications?** Are there any known side effects for the medications?

6. **Does your child grind his/her teeth?**

7. **Has your child been hospitalized since birth?**

8. **Has your child been hospitalized for any surgery?**

9. **Is your child's height and weight within the normal range for his/her age?** Do you have any concerns about height and weight?

10. **What physicians are currently taking care of your child?** Does your child have a medical diagnosis?

11. **What therapists are currently working with your child?** Has there been any prior testing for speech/language skills and feeding skills?

Source: Bruns & Thompson, 2011. Used with permission.

Oral Structures/Movement Worksheet

Name:	Birthday:
Age:	Date:
Diagnosis:	

1. Oral Structures: Appearance at Rest

A. Lips:

B. Gums:

C. Tongue:

D. Cheeks:

E. Upper Jaw:

F. Lower Jaw:

G. Hard Palate:

H. Soft Palate:

I. Teeth:

2. Oral Structures During Movement: I: (imitation) S: (spontaneous)
(Note asymmetries, movement patterns, and ability to produce separate movements)

A. Lower Jaw/Upper Jaw
   1. Open mouth:

   2. Smile:

   3. Open/close mouth:

Source: Revised from Flanagan, 2008. Used with permission.

Oral Structures/Movement Worksheet (*cont.*)

2. Oral Structures During Movement: I: (imitation) S: (spontaneous) (*cont.*)

B. Lips
   4. Pucker:

   5. Blow:

   6. Hum:

   7. Oo-ee:

   8. Lip smack:

C. Cheeks
   9. Puff out cheeks:

D. Tongue
   10. Tongue out (with mouth open):

   11. Tongue out/in (with mouth open):

   12. Tongue tip up inside of mouth:

   13. Tongue tip to upper lip:

   14. Tongue tip down inside of mouth:

Oral Structures/Movement Worksheet (*cont.*)

**2. Oral Structures During Movement: I: (imitation) S: (spontaneous)
(*cont.*)**

D. Tongue (*cont.*)
15. Tongue tip to chin:

16. Tongue side to side to mouth corners:

17. Tongue side to side to lower teeth:

18. Tongue side to side to cheeks:

19. Tongue side to side to upper teeth:

20. Tongue click:

3. Oral and Postural Muscle Tone

A. Facial tone:

B. Lingual tone:

C. Body tone:

4. Breathing

A. Oral breather:

B. Nasal breather:

Oral Structures/Movement Worksheet (*cont.*)

5. Oral Sensitivity

A. Gag reflex:

B. Reaction to oral sensory input:

C. Food texture/temperature:

D. Food texture/temperature:

6. Descriptions of Movements While:

A. Drinking:
   1. Breast/Bottle:

   2. Cup:

      a. Lips:

      b. Tongue:

      c. Jaw:

      d. Swallow:

   3. Straw:

B. Spoon Food:
   1. Lips:

   2. Tongue:

   3. Jaw:

   4. Swallow:

7. Classification of Movement Patterns:

A. Typical Development:

B. Reflexive/Primitive:

C. Delayed:

D. Atypical:

Glossary

Apraxia: A motor speech disorder involving difficulty planning the movements and sequences of sounds for speech production.

ARK Probe: An oral motor tool used to provide oral awareness and discrimination to the tongue, lips, and cheeks.

Atypical development: Skills or behaviors that would not be seen in the child's typical peers of the same chronological age.

Auditory system: The sense of hearing through which we receive and process information.

Autism spectrum disorder (ASD): A developmental disorder that is characterized by deficits in social interactions, language, communication and play, with stereotypic, repetitive behaviors and a narrow range of interests.

Autonomic nervous system: Part of the peripheral nervous system that controls such functions as heart rate, respiration rate, digestion, and perspiration.

Aversion: A desire to avoid something or someone.

Cheek/lip retraction: Pulling back of the cheeks and lips due to increased muscle tone restricting movement.

Chew tube: A solid, washable, nontoxic tube used to facilitate chewing and biting.

Delayed development: Development of the same skills as typical peers but at a slower rate.

Distal: Away from the middle or center of the body.

Dysarthria: A motor speech disorder that involves difficulty with speech due to incoordination or weakness of the musculature.

Enterocolitis: An inflammation of the digestive tract.

Esophagitis: An inflammation of the esophagus.

Esophagus: A muscular tube that transfers saliva, liquids, and food from the mouth to the stomach.

Fight, flight, or freeze: A hyper-alert state used for survival.

Gag reflex: A protective oral reflex in response to harmful or unknown stimuli.

Gastritis: An inflammation of the lining of the stomach.

Gastroesophageal reflux: Also known as GERD, this involves the stomach liquids going up into the throat.

Gustatory system: The sensory system for the sense of taste.

Hypersensitivity: Over-reactive to sensation.

Hypertonia: High or increased muscle tone.

Hyposensitivity: Under-reactive to sensation.

Hypotonia: Low or decreased muscle tone.

Inhibition: A mental process imposing restraint upon behavior.

Isometric exercise: An exercise used to train the strength of a muscle or muscle group.

Jaw clenching: Tightly closing the jaw in a clamped position.

Joint compression: An activity that provides input to the proprioceptive system and may help the child to feel calm.

Mobility: Capable of moving.

Modulate: The facilitation of some neural messages while inhibiting others when producing a response.

Motor planning: The ability to cognitively organize and produce a sequence of novel movements.

Munching: An early chewing pattern that combines the phasic bite reflex with rhythmical, non-stereotypical vertical tongue movement to the palate.

Muscle tone: A state of tension or readiness of a muscle to respond to a stretch.

Nuk Massage Brush: An oval-shaped brush produced for infants to help them become accustomed to teeth-brushing. It is frequently used by therapists to provide oral stimulation.

Olfactory system: The sensory system for the sense of smell.

Oral apraxia: A disorder involving difficulty with the production of volitional oral movements such as sticking out your tongue or licking your lips, even when capable of producing these movements.

Oral-motor: The ability to purposefully move the lips, tongue, cheeks, palate, and jaw with stability, grading, and separation due to an intact sensory-motor feedback system.

Oral structures: The lips, cheeks, tongue, teeth, jaw, gums, and palate.

Papillae: The end organs on the body of the tongue for the sense of taste.

Primitive movements: Movements seen in the infant during the first 3–4 months of development (e.g., oral reflexes).

Proprioceptive system: The sensory system that gives us information from the sensory receptors in our muscles and joints. This system gives information about what the body is doing in space.

Proximal: Located toward the center of the body.

Reflexes: Involuntary movements to specific sensory input that are present at birth. Many of these reflexes become integrated at different times in development.

Register: To notice and pay attention to.

Sensory input: The information that goes from the sensory receptors to the brain.

Sensory integration: The ability to organize and use sensory information to interact with the environment.

Tactile defensiveness: A condition due to difficulty modulating sensory input that causes the child to react negatively to touch.

Tactile system: The system where sensory input is received by the sensory receptors in the skin and sent to the central nervous system.

Tongue retraction: A pulling back of the tongue into the mouth. The tip of the tongue may be held up against the palate.

Tongue thrust: A forceful forward movement of the tongue.

Vestibular system: The sensory system located in the inner ear that registers changes in gravity and influences muscle tone, movement, and balance.

CPSIA information can be obtained
at www.ICGtesting.com
Printed in the USA
FSOW04n1516280416
19775FS

9 781942 197133